Steps
to Better
Writing

Steps to Better Writing

A Guide to the Process

LEA LANE

ST. MARTIN'S PRESS
New York

book design: Judith Woracek

ISBN: 0-312-76171-6

ACKNOWLEDGMENT

"The U.S. Family" by Sar A. Levitan © 1981 by The New York Times
Company. Reprinted by permission.

To Monica

Preface

"What is written without effort is in general read without pleasure," Dr. Johnson said, and surely he spoke the truth. Writing well is seldom easy. Effort, however, is not the whole secret; one doesn't necessarily write better just by working harder, by expending more and more undirected energy, as many inexperienced writers try to do. The writer needs to understand that any writing project involves a number of different kinds of work—what this book calls *steps*; that, although variations are possible, these steps have a logical and practical sequence; and that if part of writing well is mastering skills, another part is managing time, giving each step its due. In particular, beginning writers need to know that the most important work is usually done before and after a draft is written. With apologies to Dr. Johnson, the student who learns these things and applies them will discover that the result is papers read with more pleasure and in general written with *less* effort.

To help students achieve such proficiency and reap those rewards is the purpose of *Steps to Better Writing*. The book has grown out of my experiences as a teacher of beginning and advanced writing courses in a large public city college and two small private colleges; as director of numerous practical writing workshops for employees of corporations; and as a professional writer for magazines, newspapers, and films. Whatever may be the book's shortcomings, and no doubt it has many, it has at least the virtue that all the advice in it has proved thrice useful—to students, to people on the job, and to the author herself.

The writing process is not simple, not straightforward, and not fully understood—and yet I have sought to ensure that my presentation of the process will be all of those things, especially the last. Students make the greatest gains in control of their writing when they view the writing process as a sequence of clearly defined steps that can be mastered one at a time. That is how I present the process in this book: a series of seven steps that leads from first thoughts to final recopying. It is essential, however, that students never lose sight of the whole process while concentrating on particular steps. For example, part of what makes drafting free and easy (if all goes well) is the writer's awareness *while drafting* that opportunities for revision are "scheduled" later in the process. Similarly, the trials of prewriting are made bearable by the writer's expectation of a consequent ease in drafting, among other rewards.

Descriptions of the writing process often divide it into the phases of invention, writing a draft, and revision. I call these phases—and the three main sections of the book that are devoted to them—*Prewriting*, *Freewriting*, and *Rewriting*. The rhyme and repetition help students keep all three phases of the process in mind at once, and the presence of *-writing* in every term (as well as the absence of *writing* as a free-standing word anywhere in the series) helps emphasize that the phases are all intrinsic to writing, that they are not the prelude, the "thing itself," and what you do "afterwards."

Please note that this book uses the term *freewriting* in a quite different sense from the one in which it is used by Peter Elbow and others. Here the term refers to the drafting phase, whereas Elbow uses it to refer to a particular kind of timed-writing exercise in which, as Elbow stresses, the process is everything and the written product is purely incidental. At the risk of some initial misperceptions (corrected here, I hope), I went ahead with my own usage because the word stresses so perfectly the things I wish to emphasize: the freedom, the ease, the flow of words and ideas that characterize the drafting phase at its best, when earlier steps have been given due attention and later steps are borne in mind so that perfection is not the immediate (and paralyzing) goal. In short, I like the word for many of the same reasons Elbow likes it, but I employ it differently.

The fourth, and last, section of *Steps to Better Writing* is a concise guide to writing research papers. Using the same seven-step sequence presented by the previous sections, it provides a final illustration of how a writer moves from prewriting to freewriting to rewriting in the composition of an interesting and effective paper. Sample notes, an outline, two successive drafts, and the finished paper are included.

With a final nod to Dr. Johnson, who started this preface, we may say that what is written without pleasure is likely to be read only with effort. The pleasures in writing this book have been many, but none has been greater than that of working with the help of so many wise and generous people. I am deeply indebted to Joan E. Hartman, College of Staten Island; Lorraine Murphy, University of Dayton; Sharon Niederman, Metropolitan State College; Ted Romoser, Lane Community College; Marilyn Rosen, Borough of Manhattan Community College; and Grace P. Volick, C. W. Post College. All of them read the manuscript and made invaluable suggestions for its improvement. Whatever faults remain are of course my responsibility alone. I owe special thanks to Tom Broadbent, John Francis, Patricia Mansfield, Nancy Perry, and Charles Thurlow of St. Martin's Press. Finally, I am grateful to Ernestine Opie, for support; Bea Bussey, for thoughtful, generous assistance; Rand and Cary, for their love; and Fred, for all of these things.

Lea Lane

Contents

Preface   vii

Introduction   1

PHASE ONE: PREWRITING   5

Step One: Choose a Topic   7

Interest   8
Familiarity   9
Limitations   9
Reader   11
Purpose   13
Controlling Idea   14
Summary   16

Step Two: Gather Information   17

Experience   18
Observation   18
Brainstorming   19

Reading   22
Experts   26
   Interviewing in Person and by Telephone   26
   Interviewing by Mail   27
Television and Radio   28
Summary   29

Step Three: Organize   30

Patterns of Development   31
   Narration   32
   Description   32
   Process Instruction and Process Explanation   34
   Analysis   35
   Classification   36
   Comparison and Contrast   38
   Analogy   40
   Definition   42
   Illustration (Exemplification)   43
   Cause and Effect   45
   Argument   47
Order   51
   Kinds of Order   53
   CLIMACTIC ORDER   53
   CHRONOLOGICAL ORDER AND FLASHBACK   54
   SPATIAL ORDER   55
Coordinating Your Plan   56
Writing an Outline   59
   Informal Outline   59
   Formal Outline   63
Summary   66

PHASE TWO: FREEWRITING   67

Step Four: Write a Draft   69

Warm Up   69
   Equipment   69
   Environment   70
   Preparation   70
Let Loose   71
Cool Down   74
Summary   74

PHASE THREE: REWRITING   75

Step Five: Revise   77

Mark Up the Draft   78
Tips for Revising   78
Use a Checklist   79
Content   80
Organization   82
Paragraphs   85
Opening, Ending, Title   94
Summary   98

Step Six: Refine   99

Mark Your Draft   100
Use a Checklist   100
Style   101
Words   107
Sentences   115
Mechanics   132
Summary   136

Step Seven: Recopy   137

Be Neat   137
Follow a Format   138
Proofread   138
Summary   139

THE RESEARCH PAPER   141

Step One: Choose a Topic   142
Step Two: Gather Information   143
  Plan   143
  Use the Library   144
  DETERMINE KINDS OF SOURCES   144
  FIND SOURCES   145
  LIST AND EVALUATE SOURCES   147
  READ AND TAKE NOTES   148
Step Three: Organize   150
Step Four: Write a Draft   152
  Quotations   152
  Paraphrase   154
  Summary   154

Step Five: Revise   155
Step Six: Refine   155
Step Seven: Recopy   155

  Add Notes   155
  Add the Bibliography   156
  Determine Formats for Bibliography and Footnotes   157
  BOOKS   157
  GOVERNMENT PUBLICATION   160
  ARTICLES IN PERIODICALS   161
  OTHER SOURCE MATERIALS   164
  Determine the Final Format   166

Sample Research Paper   167

Index   201

Steps
to Better
Writing

Introduction

Do you think you write well? If not, it probably isn't because you're lazy or stupid or you don't care. Perhaps it's because you think that writing should be easy and natural, like talking—that it shouldn't require much practice. But writing is a skill, like swimming or playing the piano. Without instruction and practice, most people can't do it at all, let alone do it well.

What is good writing anyway?

Good writing is clear. The reader can easily understand it.

Good writing conserves energy—the reader's. It lets the reader quickly see the connection between facts and conclusions, and it uses only necessary words. (Of course, saving the reader's energy can require lots of the writer's.)

Good writing gives good value. It's packed with information and even insight, with facts and ideas the reader never knew or never considered from the writer's point of view.

Good writing is responsible. Every opinion or generalization is supported with evidence.

To sum up, good writing doesn't confuse or deceive the reader; rather, it informs and enlightens.

A swimmer doesn't enter a swimming meet badly out of shape; a pianist doesn't perform without rehearsing. But though writing well is important for success in college and after, you may have little idea how to go about it. You probably know something about putting sentences together, what a paragraph is, and how to punctuate and spell—but not much about the *process* of writing.

Steps to Better Writing offers a logical, step-by-step guide to the writing process. It divides the process into three phases: preparing to write a first draft ("prewriting"), writing the draft ("freewriting"), and converting the draft into a finished piece of prose ("rewriting").

During prewriting, you are a *thinker*. You gather and analyze facts and ideas, develop them, and put them in a logical order. During freewriting, you are a *writer*. You concentrate on getting your thoughts down on paper. Finally, during rewriting, you are a *critic*. You read what you have written, analyze how fully and effectively it expresses your thoughts, and concentrate on improving it.

To make the writing process still easier to understand and study, the three phases are divided into seven steps:

Phase One: Prewriting

Step One: Choose a topic.

Step Two: Gather information.

Step Three: Organize.

Phase Two: Freewriting

Step Four: Write a draft.

Phase Three: Rewriting

Step Five: Revise.

Step Six: Refine.

Step Seven: Recopy.

Practice these steps one by one, just as athletes practice each aspect of their sport independently. Be sure to do the exercises that accompany them. As you adapt the steps to your own writing habits, you may find that some of them overlap or combine. For instance, you might freewrite sentences while discovering facts and ideas, or think of a plan of organization as you're choosing a topic. That's how many people write.

Use the seven steps for all your writing, whether it's a short letter or a term paper. Soon they will become a natural part of the way you write.

Following the seven steps will not require you to take more time to write. In fact, you will probably save time, because the steps present a complex process in manageable sections. You'll know exactly what you have to do. You won't have to stop and start, stare at the ceiling, or chew your nails in frustration.

But you will have to learn to budget your writing time. If you have half an hour to answer an essay question, you might spend five to ten minutes prewriting, ten to fifteen minutes freewriting, and the remaining time rewriting.

Some types of writing, such as research papers, require more time for prewriting; on others, such as essays based on personal experience, you may spend most of your time rewriting. With practice, you will learn to estimate how long you should work on each phase of writing; ultimately, you'll be able to budget your writing time almost instinctively.

Steps to Better Writing focuses on the type of writing most useful in college and at work. It's called "practical writing" because it is used in practical situations for practical reasons: letters, memos, articles, reports, term papers, job applications, proposals, research papers, speeches. Practical writing does not have to be brilliant or artistic. It does have to be clear and effective. It must do what the writer wants it to do. Using the seven steps can help you achieve those goals. You can learn to write better. Indeed, you can learn to write well.

Phase One: Prewriting

You opened the box, took out a brand new Skipman headset radio, inserted the batteries, donned the headphones, and switched on the radio. Nothing happened. You checked the instructions to make sure you had done everything right—and you had.

Now you want to write a letter of complaint to the manufacturer, the Corporal Electric Company. Do you rush to your desk and dash off a letter filled with threats? No. You must make a few decisions first.

To whom are you going to address the letter? You decide to write to the customer service manager. What are you going to ask the manager for? You will request a Skipman that works properly or a refund of your money. You will enclose the bill of sale and the one-year warranty. Before you start writing, you remember why you bought the radio—you own other electronic equipment manufactured by Corporal Electric and have always been satisfied with the company's products and services. You jot down a few key words to include in the letter—words such as *immediate action*, *replace*, and *refund*.

When you make decisions such as these, you are prewriting—preparing to write. Prewriting is the backbone of writing; it supports the whole structure.

There are three key steps to prewriting:

Step One: Choose a topic.
Step Two: Gather information.
Step Three: Organize.

You should take each of these prewriting steps whenever you write.

To produce a mighty book you must choose a mighty theme.

HERMAN MELVILLE

Step 1: Choose a Topic

Sometimes, would you rather do anything—arrange your records in alphabetical order, sweep the dustballs from under your bed—than begin writing? Yet, at other times, do you sit right down and fill up page after page while the mail lies unopened and your pepperoni pizza grows cold?

The difference may be your choice of topic. Writing involves making choices, and the first and perhaps the most important is deciding what to write about. This step doesn't require much time, yet it's often rushed or skipped altogether. As a result, essays fizzle, reports lie unfinished, and research papers flop. With the right topic, they might have dazzled.

Sometimes, the choice of topic may be limited ("Write an essay in answer to one of the following questions. . ."), or broad ("Write about someone you admire"), or wide open ("Write a letter to a friend"). At other times, you may not have a choice at all. You may be assigned a topic like "Keep an hourly record of your activities from the time you wake up Monday until 9 P.M. Saturday" or "Describe the mating habits of palmetto weevils."

In some apparently no-choice situations, you might muster your courage and request another topic. Instructors often encourage such initiative and respond well to it. When the topic choice is yours, however, you should consider several factors before choosing—interest, familiarity, limitations, reader, purpose, and controlling idea.

INTEREST

Too many students waste their time writing about things that they consider uninteresting. They procrastinate, suffer, and mutter, "I hate writing," when what they really hate is their topics.

Why do students sometimes choose topics that don't interest them? Maybe they wait until the last minute to write; then they commit themselves to the first idea that flashes across their minds because they are so relieved to have found a topic.

Unfortunately, many students eliminate topics they would *like* to write about for topics they believe they *should* write about. But if they liked what they were writing about, they'd probably write better. And a well-written paper on "The Legend of Elvis" is just as worthwhile as a well-written paper on "The Legend of Edison."

When writers have free choice, they can usually find a topic they want to write about. But even when a topic is assigned, they should be able to find some aspect of it that interests them. For example, if you're asked to write a paper on an aspect of Boston and you're not enthusiastic, don't give up. Write down "Boston." Now stretch your mind. What about Boston interests you? The Red Sox? The Tea Party? The Kennedys? Harvard? Baked beans? Write down all associations that come to mind. By free-associating, you should find at least one interesting aspect of the topic, and you may be surprised at where it leads. For instance, the Boston Tea Party might lead you to think about the waterfront development on Boston harbor, an example of the successful recycling of old buildings for new uses.

EXERCISE 1-1

Write a list of five facts or ideas that interest you. Use it when you want to select a writing topic. Add others as you think of them.

EXERCISE 1-2

Skim the articles in a newspaper or magazine. Then choose five articles whose topics do not particularly interest you. Free-associate, and write down the aspects of each topic that do interest you enough to write about.

FAMILIARITY

Suppose you're asked to write an essay describing a natural setting. Although you live in Aspen, you're fascinated with beaches, so you decide to write about Malibu. However, all you know about Malibu is that it's sandy, located in California, and fringed by expensive houses. That's certainly not enough information for an essay.

A topic that interests you *and* that you know something about would be a better choice. If you write about Aspen in autumn, you could describe the gold leaves shimmering against a cobalt blue sky, the sudden cold of a mountain nightfall, and the smell of roasted chestnuts from cabin chimneys settling over the streets.

When you don't have the time or opportunity to research a topic, it's important to write about the familiar: what you experience, feel, imagine, understand, and know. Your experiences and perceptions are unique. Drawing on details stored in your memory can make your writing vivid, forceful, and natural. And don't overlook everyday happenings as possible topics; what is familiar to you may be unusual, even exotic, to your readers.

EXERCISE 1-3

List at least ten areas in which you consider yourself knowledgeable—for example, academic subjects, hobbies, work, and travel.

LIMITATIONS

Consider three limiting factors before deciding on a topic:

- time available
- length of assignment
- resources available

If you were writing a book in your spare time, with no deadline, no particular page length, and extensive resources, then you could write *The History of the Galaxies*. But if you had a three-page paper due on Friday and could only get to the library on Thursday, then your topic selection would be greatly affected. You would have to narrow the topic to one that you

could cover in the assigned number of pages and with the time and resources available to you.

Much writing is vague and overgeneral simply because the topic is too
large to handle within the given limitations. If your topic is too broad, your
writing will be rushed, incomplete, and haphazard. Moreover, you are
likely to omit details and specific examples, and you might not know where
to begin or end.

How do you know whether your topic is too broad for the time available? Use your good judgment. You'd know immediately, for example, that
thirty minutes would not be enough time to write an essay about American
film. However, you could narrow the topic to fit the time limit by using a
diagram like the following:

American film——American film comedians——
Charlie Chaplin
Mae West
Goldie Hawn
Woody Allen

Does any of these topics seem workable? If not, pull out the most promising one, and break it down further:

Woody Allen——Allen's film roles ——Allen's performance in *Manhattan*

Or, branch off in a different direction:

American film——American film musicals——
The Wizard of Oz
My Fair Lady
Grease
Annie

"American film" can be narrowed into many different topics using this
kind of diagram. At least one should be a topic you can cover within half an
hour.

A word of caution: if you carry the diagram too far, you may end up
with a topic that's too narrow—one that's either not interesting or not complex enough to write about. For example, if you've narrowed the second
diagram to "Woody Allen's facial expressions in *Manhattan*," you've probably gone too far.

Another kind of topic that is too narrow is one that merely states a fact:
"Woody Allen lives in New York," or "*Manhattan* was released in 1978."
These "topics" are dead ends; they leave no room for discussion.

Your topic should start you thinking of facts and ideas, of things you
want to explain and points you want to make. "Woody Allen lives in New
York" and "*Manhattan* was released in 1978" might be combined into a
more fruitful topic: "Only a New Yorker could have written *Manhattan*."
That statement gives you something to think and write about.

EXERCISE 1-4

Assume that you have one hour to write a short paper and you are unable to get to a library. Which of the following topics would you be able to write about? Mark *S* next to those that are suitable, *B* next to those that are too broad, *N* next to those that are too narrow, and *R* next to those that require research.

1. New Year's Eve parties around the world
2. Quaker New Year's Eve parties in eighteenth-century Pennsylvania
3. my last New Year's Eve
4. books
5. my cat Rover
6. I am ten pounds overweight.
7. The Shah of Iran died in Egypt.
8. sleeping patterns of fleas
9. the life of Calvin Coolidge
10. some funny camp songs

EXERCISE 1-5

Using the type of diagram shown on page 10, narrow each of the following general topics.

1. the United States
2. baseball
3. fashion
4. religion

Choose one of the narrowed topics, and using a diagram, narrow it still further. Now consider all of the topics. Which ones could be adequately covered in a one-hour class assignment? Which would require a long paper? Which would be too narrow to write about?

READER

Who is your reader? This is one of the first things you must determine, because it affects not only your choice of topic but the whole writing process. In college courses, your readers are your instructors and sometimes your fellow students. But your reader can also be the potential employer who'll read your job application or the friend who receives your personal letter.

Sometimes, the reader assigns the topic—for example, teachers of college courses, job supervisors, and evaluators of project proposals. But whether or not you are free to choose your topic, keep in mind who the reader will be.

For example, if you plan to write an article on the benefits of vegetarian diets for a typical audience of American readers, you should consider that this audience will consist mostly of people who are not vegetarians but who care about their health and their diets; who know a few basic facts about nutrition (and quite a few nonfacts) but not what you have to tell them; and who may find vegetarianism unusual but not repelling. In other words, even if your readers do not plan to become vegetarians, they probably will be interested in the information you have to offer.

However, if you are writing about the benefits of vegetarianism for members of the American Cattlemen's Association, you will probably find these readers hostile to the very notion. You do not have to compromise your own principles or change your point of view. But to keep the attention of this audience—and to convince them of the validity of your information—you do have to build a very strong case. No doubt you will have to provide evidence for this audience that you would not have needed for the other audience, and you may also need to present your information in a different order.

To analyze your audience, consider:

- *Vital statistics*
  Age, sex, race, nationality, occupation.
- *Background*
  Education, social and economic class, religious and political views.
- *Interests and viewpoints*
  What interests the readers about my topic?
  What do they know about my topic?
  How will they probably react to my ideas about the topic?
  What do they know about me, and how will that affect their reaction?

With a clear idea of your audience, you can make effective decisions at every step of the writing process. You can decide what information is too basic or too difficult, what you can simply state and what you will have to explain or prove, and even how best to organize and express your ideas. And when you've finished writing a draft, you can read it from your reader's point of view—a great help in deciding what to revise.

What if you're unable to learn much about your readers? For example, you're writing an article for a magazine published for the so-called general audience. In this case, assume that the readers are reasonably interested in your topic and as intelligent as you, but that they know less about the topic than you do.

EXERCISE 1-6

Examine the following lists. Which topic seems most appropriate for each reader?

Reader	Topic
doctor	religion in America
nun	making the most of leisure time
corporation president	choosing a career
retired fire fighter	union power
teenager	the American medical system

Now find an aspect of each topic that would interest one of the *other* readers (use a narrowing diagram if you wish).

EXERCISE 1-7

Select an article from a newspaper or magazine. Then choose an article on the same topic from each of four other newspapers or magazines. Describe the readership of each publication, and show how each article is written for that audience.

PURPOSE

Another question you must consider is *why* you are writing about your topic. What is your purpose? If you have your purpose clearly in mind, you should be able to state it in a sentence. And the more precisely you are able to state your purpose before you begin writing, the greater the likelihood that your paper will succeed. A sharply focused statement of purpose will give direction to your writing.

For instance, suppose you are interested in writing about the topic "vegetarian diets." Fine, but "I want to write about vegetarian diets" would not be a very useful statement of purpose; it is just too vague. The following statements of purpose are better because each one begins to suggest a direction in which your writing might proceed.

I want to describe the different kinds of vegetarian diets.

I want to explain how to set up an ideal vegetarian diet.

I want to persuade readers to switch to vegetarian diets.

I want to show readers why vegetarian diets are unnatural.

I want to describe the ideal vegetarian diet for people who hate vegetables.

Often, to persuade a reader you may also have to explain, and to keep the reader reading you may have to entertain. That's fine. But first establish your purpose for writing and state it in a sentence. Then you can keep that statement of purpose in mind throughout the writing process.

EXERCISE 1-8

For each of the following topics, write a statement of purpose in sentence form.

1. television game shows
2. the death penalty
3. energy conservation
4. the space shuttle
5. college sports

Now do the same for five topics of your own.

CONTROLLING IDEA

Sometimes your statement of purpose may be sufficient to guide you as you gather and organize your information (the next steps we'll be considering). This is especially likely if your purpose for writing is purely to inform, as it often is in, for instance, reporting events, giving instructions, or explaining processes:

> I want to give an account of yesterday's Student Senate meeting.
>
> I want to provide instructions for giving a hypodermic injection.
>
> I want to explain tides.

Very often, however, and especially if your purpose is to convince your reader of something, you will find it indispensable to formulate a *controlling idea* to help guide you through the rest of the writing process. This controlling idea (sometimes called a *thesis*) is the main point your piece of writing will make, the proposition you will be stating and supporting with examples, illustrations, and evidence. As with your statement of purpose, you should put the controlling idea into a sentence, write it down, and keep it before you as you work.

The more precise you can make the controlling idea, the more it will help you. Suppose, for example, that the purpose of your writing is *to persuade readers to switch to vegetarian diets*. Your controlling idea might then be:

> The advantages of vegetarian diets far outweigh the disadvantages.

Note that your task is now much more clearly defined than it was when you had only your statement of purpose. You know that your next job is to compile a list of advantages and a list of disadvantages.

A controlling idea helps you in every phase of the writing process. In prewriting, it helps you decide which facts and ideas are relevant to what you want to say and which are not. In freewriting, it will keep your mind focused as you write your first draft. And, in rewriting, it will help you judge whether what you've written is actually what you wanted to write, or whether you've failed to make your point.

In some cases, you won't be sure of the controlling idea until you've gathered some ideas and facts about your topic. At that point, you may clarify or even change your statement of purpose—and your controlling idea as well. If you learn, for example, that vegetarianism is less healthy and practical for city-dwellers than for other people, you might not want to persuade *everyone* that "the advantages of vegetarian diets far outweigh the disadvantages." You might change your controlling idea to: "Vegetarian diets can easily be maintained as a part of healthy country living."

EXERCISE 1-9

Return to the statements of purpose you wrote in Exercise 1-8. For as many of these statements as possible, write a sentence stating a controlling idea. Were you able to provide a controlling idea for all of them? If not, why not?

Professional tip. Make notes on your topic, limitations, reader, purpose, and controlling idea, and keep them in a handy file as you move through the steps of the writing process. Keep a separate file for each new writing project. Or, do your thinking on paper, in a journal. Then you can remind yourself not only what you decided but also why.

SUMMARY

In Step One—choose a topic—you should:

- Choose an interesting topic.
- When possible, choose a familiar topic.
- Be aware of your limitations in time, length, and resources.
- Analyze your audience.
- Decide on your purpose for writing about the topic.
- State your controlling idea, if appropriate.

I only ask for information.

CHARLES DICKENS

Step 2: Gather Information

Once you have chosen a topic, your next step is to gather information and ideas about that topic. How much time and effort you spend depends on what you are writing about and how much you know about it.

For many kinds of writing, the main—or even the only—source of information is yourself. Letters, autobiographical stories, and personal essays can be written from what you alone have experienced and observed. For instance, you can probably write a dozen pages about your childhood solely from memory. And if you want to write an entertaining essay about hot fudge sundaes, you can also draw from experience—or you can spend a few delectable minutes at an ice cream parlor doing research. On the other hand, writing about the history of chocolate or fiber electronics in telecommunications may require several days in the library, consulting dozens of sources.

Most practical writing, however, does not require you to search through card catalogs, library stacks, and multiple sources. Instead, you will often find the information you need in your own head, or in the heads of others, or perhaps in an essay or book that you have on your shelf.

At the end of this book, there is a section on the research paper (pages 141–199). If you are assigned a paper that requires extensive research, be sure to read this section before you tackle the assignment.

EXPERIENCE

The most vivid and convincing writing often comes from your direct experience. In fact, such experience is sometimes essential to a topic. For instance, you can read up on stock car racing and write an accurate report about it. But if you want to describe how it feels to drive in a race, then you have to write from experience. And you don't have to be A. J. Foyt to write about the excitement and fear of driving; your own experience on the back roads can give you plenty to write about. If you haven't raced, write about something you have experienced—perhaps taking the test for your driver's license or going on a weekend trip in your new car.

Even when your purpose does not require it, personal experience usually brings a piece of writing to life. So make notes on unusual or stimulating things that happen to you; you may be able to use some of them in your writing.

EXERCISE 2-1

Select five experiences you've had during the last year that seem interesting enough to write a personal essay about.

OBSERVATION

If you were in the grandstand at the Indianapolis 500, you would have taken in many sights and sounds that never got reported in the newspapers. The multicolored cars taking the turns high or low, the frenzied discipline of the pit crews, the response of the crowd—these are not news, but they are all part of the auto-racing experience.

In all kinds of writing, from a description of a sports event to a report of a scientific experiment, observation is crucial. You can't rely solely on what other people say they have seen; you must also give readers your own perceptions.

Unfortunately, many people are poor observers. They walk along the street with their eyes on the pavement; when they travel, they read to pass the time. Good writers, however, keep their senses of sight, sound, smell, taste, and touch open wide, taking in everything that might someday fit into their writing. Often, they keep a notepad handy and jot down observations on the spot.

When you walk to class or through your neighborhood, watch how other people walk. Listen to how they talk to each other and to the intonations of their voices; pay attention to their gestures. Notice not only the statue in the square, but the inscription on its base as well. Look out the window of the bus or train at the world streaming by. It is full of fascinating things that can make your writing more alive.

EXERCISE 2-2

Based on your observations, describe in as much detail as possible one of the following topics:

1. the way my best friend dresses
2. the sound of my favorite musical group
3. the taste of the food I like least
4. the feeling of being caught in a thunderstorm
5. the sights, sounds, and other sensations of the room where my writing class meets

---

BRAINSTORMING

Now you're ready for *brainstorming*. Brainstorming will enable you to explore your experiences and observations to discover ideas you can use in your writing. One method of brainstorming is free-association. Before you begin, write down your topic and statement of purpose and also your controlling idea, if there is one. Then, keeping in mind your purpose and controlling idea, list everything you can think of concerning your topic. Jot down key words, ideas, or phrases relating to it. Don't worry about grammar, or order, or the possible irrelevance of your entries. Keep at it until you can't think of another thing.

If you were writing a paper on vegetarian diets, your brainstorming list might look like this:

Topic: Vegetarian diets

Purpose: I want to persuade readers to switch to vegetarian diets.

Controlling idea: The advantages of vegetarian diets far outweigh the disadvantages.

Advantages	*Disadvantages*
Less expensive	Protein and other vitamin deficiencies
Less fat	Hard to adhere to in a meat-eating society
Less cholesterol	Diet not as varied
You don't kill animals	Looked upon as cultist
You won't get trichinosis	Tend to get self-righteous
You can grow your own food	May need vitamin supplements
Fresher food	Tend to get anemia
Less chance of heart disease	Complex combinations of recipes needed
Grazing animals can harm	Lack of texture, taste
the environment	
Fuel conservation	
Need less transportation	
Water conservation	
Less water pollution	
Fewer chemicals necessary	
to preserve vegetables,	
fewer cancerous agents	

(You've probably noticed that some of the notes in each column are quite similar. That's all right. Don't slow yourself down trying to prevent repetition. You can take care of it later.)

Another brainstorming technique is to ask yourself *Who? What? When? Where? Why?* and *How?*—which journalists call the "Five *W*'s and *H*." You could first make a brainstorming list by free-association, then use the questions to bring out any details that might have escaped you. And if you want to write about a general topic with many aspects or if you haven't yet established a clear statement of purpose, you could *start* with the Five *W*'s and *H*. Use them to explore your topic. You could then free-associate to develop some of the specific points. For example:

Topic: Television talk shows.

Purpose: I want to explain why television talk shows are so popular.

Who?

Who are the major talk-show hosts? Johnny Carson, Merv Griffin, Phil Donahue, David Letterman, William F. Buckley (look up others in *TV Guide*).

Who are typical talk-show guests? Show-business stars—singers, comedians, actors; also authors of books, people in the news. What kinds of people don't appear on talk shows?

Who watches talk shows? (Try to find out if there have been any surveys.)

Who sponsors them? (There may be no pattern. Check.)

What?

What are the most popular talk-show formats? Opening monologue? Number of guests? Amount of time per guest? Audience questions or participation? Does host discuss with guests or just ask questions?

What are the most popular talk shows? (Look for ratings information.)

What are the different kinds of talk shows? Entertainment, current events, local, issue-oriented, highbrow—what else? Are *Today, Good Morning America,* and other news-oriented shows talk shows or news?

What are talk-show hosts paid? Are the guests paid? Isn't a talk show one of the cheapest kinds of television programs to produce?

When?

When are particular shows telecast? Weekday mornings, weekday afternoons—for people who are home during the day? Late at night? Weekends?

When are the shows videotaped? What time of day? How many per day? How many days or weeks before they go on the air?

When did television talk shows begin? (Need to look up.)

Where?

Where are talk shows videotaped? New York, Los Angeles, Chicago—where else? How does this affect the show?

Where are they telecast? Are there some parts of the country where you can't see Donahue or Letterman or Griffin or Buckley?

Why?

Why are talk shows so popular? For example, why do I watch Johnny Carson so regularly?

Why are some talk shows on commercial television while others are on PBS? Listenership, sponsorship—anything else?

Why do guests agree to appear on talk shows? Why do some people refuse?

A general "why"—find out the reasons behind the other four W's. Why is *The Tonight Show* so successful in the ratings? Is it Johnny Carson, or the guests, or the format, or the broadcast schedule, or what?

How?

How does a talk show get put together? Choice of guests, preparation of questions, writing the introductions and monologues (any rehearsal?), prepping the guests, prepping the host, the audience (laugh and applause cues?), actually producing and videotaping the show, editing (bleeps?), etc.

How do the talk shows differ from each other? Merv Griffin from Johnny Carson, Donahue from Buckley, etc.

After this kind of brainstorming session, you would realize that "television talk shows" is a very big topic—too big for a short essay. Although you could answer some of your questions from personal experience and observation (and perhaps a look through *TV Guide*), others would require you to do research in the library. Try to choose a narrower topic that interests you and that you can handle within your limitations of time and resources, such as "major talk-show hosts." Now you can do some more brainstorming about talk-show hosts, their different styles, and what they have in common.

EXERCISE 2-3

Choose one of the topics you listed in Exercise 1-1 on page 8, and brainstorm. Free-associate for at least five minutes; then use the Five W's and H to help you discover additional ideas.

READING

One of the best ways to gather information is by reading. Through reading you can go beyond your own experience and observation, and make the best thinkers and writers work for you. Reading can provide facts, observations, and logical reasoning that you can use in your own writing. Not only can it supply you with new material; it can stimulate you to remember past experiences and to create ideas of your own.

In addition, reading can influence your purpose, your controlling idea, and even your topic. In fact, writers often get ideas for new topics from something they read.

For example, if you read a newspaper editorial in favor of restoring the military draft in peacetime, you may respond in several ways:

- *You may agree* and write an essay giving your own reasons, perhaps including some of the editorial writer's reasons.
- *You may disagree* and write an essay showing that the editorial is illogical, untrue, or irrelevant.
- *You may neither agree nor disagree* but decide to comment on the draft issue from a different perspective, such as what the draft would mean to your own life.
- *You might think of something else to write about*—for example, another traditional, long period of involuntary servitude known as "going to school."

Whenever you include information or ideas from another source in your writing, be sure to identify the source. For example:

> George Orwell argues in "Politics and the English Language" that much political writing is intentionally dishonest.

Do not plagiarize (*plagiarism* is the use of somebody else's ideas or words in your writing as if they were your own instead of giving the original author credit). When using the exact words of a source, you must set them off with quotation marks:

> Analyzing a Communist pamphlet, George Orwell says that "the writer knows more or less what he wants to say, but an accumulation of stale phrases chokes him like tea leaves blocking a sink."

When professional writers are caught plagiarizing, they are often sued for large sums of money, even if the plagiarism was accidental. Students who plagiarize don't get sued, but most colleges punish plagiarism severely. It's worth taking a little time to avoid a lot of trouble.

Professional tip. Always identify your sources, giving the author, the title of the book or other publication, the date it was published, and the page(s). As you are taking notes from a source, write this information just before or after the note itself. You may want to reread your source later. And if you use the note in your writing, you *must* be able to say where you got the fact or idea.

EXERCISE 2-4

Read the following article from the *New York Times*.

The U.S. Family

Public debate over abortions, the Equal Rights Amendment, divorce, out-of-wedlock births, and welfare has raised deep-seated concerns about the future of the American family. Almost all the ruminations on the current status and future of the family have tended to be extreme. Alarmists issue dire warnings that the family is disintegrating, while others respond with shouts of joy, welcoming the crumbling of the institution.

Both sides ought to hold the obituaries. Families, though having undergone very wrenching changes, are far more resilient than is often thought. Margaret Mead's observation some 30 years ago that the family is the "toughest institution we have" is still valid. Indeed, social and economic forces may actually buttress the family in the years ahead, though it will continue to evolve.

Despite the turbulence of the last two decades, repeated survey research shows that Americans now place top priority on family life and marriage as critical aspects of personal development and happiness. The proportion of adults who are married at some time in their lives remains at a historically high level. Americans have not soured on marriage even if fewer are willing to remain with one spouse, until death do them part. About 38 percent of first marriages by women in their mid- to late 20's will end in divorce, yet three of every four of them will remarry. The divorce rates may not fall to the low pre-1940 levels, but neither do they seem to be progressing geometrically, as is often assumed.

Married couples have not rejected parenthood. While they want fewer children, few wish to remain childless. Small increases in fertility rates have already occurred, as many women realize that motherhood is a now-or-never proposition. Medical technology has made it possible for proportionately more women to have children, even though today more women postpone motherhood. Population declines are far from a reality in this country.

A major concern has centered on children of broken homes because the number of youngsters affected by divorce has more than tripled since 1956. Yet almost 70 percent of all children still live with their natural parents, and nearly all children live with at least one parent. Children today have a much higher chance of living with either a mother or father than those in previous generations.

The average number of children per divorce has decreased as the population of divorces involving no young children has increased. Roughly half of the households headed by divorced and separated women contain no children. Recent data do not support the notion, therefore, that the number of children involved in divorce will continue to increase.

Household shifts show a far more complex pattern than simple rejection of the family. For many younger adults, the first marriage, without children, appears to be a quasi-tryout legitimized by church or state, serving as a preparatory period for the second marriage, which most often includes having children.

In the 1970's, the number of unmarried couples increased by 150 percent, to more than one million. But in most cases, cohabitation is only a period for experimentation, or a transitional way station, before an adult moves on to the more conventional family patterns. However, "living in sin" is not a recent invention. The writer Richard Lingeman found that during the 20 years before the Revolution, one-third of all births in Concord, Mass., were conceived prior to marriage, which roughly equals current rates. So much for good old puritanical New England.

Women's increased participation in the work force hardly indicates their rejection of family life. Given the impact of inflation and slower productivity growth, an increasing number of families have required a second paycheck to maintain living standards or to realize rising aspirations. While change has been slow, there are indications that working wives show a greater propensity to demand and receive a more equal role in family decisions. All this indicates some basic shifts in stereotyped sex roles. Most working women have tried to combine careers with an active family life; paid employment has not led to a rejection of marriage and motherhood, since bedroom technology has made it possible to plan parenthood around a career.

For the time being, and in the foreseeable future, the married-couple household is likely to remain the predominant family arrangement, though households are demonstrating a high degree of variation. It will require a greater degree of flexibility in public policy to cope with the diverse needs of different types of households. But there is no reason to place the family on the endangered species list.

SAR A. LEVITAN

Now answer the following questions:

1. What is Sar A. Levitan's topic?
2. Can you tell what Levitan's purpose was in writing this essay?
3. Does the essay have a controlling idea? If so, what is it?
4. What audience was the essay written for?
5. Do you think Levitan wrote this essay from his personal experience and observation, or did he use other sources? If you think he used other sources, can you identify them?

Use Levitan's essay to help you choose a topic of your own. Find a controlling idea, then gather information both from your own experience and observation and from Levitan's essay.

EXPERTS

Today almost everyone seems to be an authority on some subject, from acupuncture to Zen. Universities, hospitals, corporations, and government agencies are filled with specialists. All of them are experts who could help you add current facts, anecdotes, and informed opinions to your writing. And don't forget your next-door neighbor who's an expert on growing succulents, or your friend who develops film, or your classmate who worked for a publisher last summer.

The most efficient way to consult experts is to interview them—in person, by telephone, or by mail. To get the most out of an interview, you must be well prepared. Gather as much information as you can by brainstorming and reading; find out as much as you can about the person you're going to interview. Use the Five *W*'s and *H* to invent questions. Then choose the ones that are most important to your writing project and which your expert is qualified to answer. Write them down.

Interviewing in Person and by Telephone

If you want to interview an expert in person or over the phone, call or write to make an appointment, suggesting several dates and times for the expert to choose from. Sometimes it's useful to send your questions ahead of time, so the expert can think over what to say. And, if an interview isn't possible, you might ask the expert to suggest other experts or helpful books and articles.

Start the interview on time. Try to be both courteous and relaxed; this puts the respondent at ease. Make sure that you've allowed enough time for your prepared questions all to be answered, with a bit of time left over for some unstructured talk. Unexpected facts and spontaneous stories can be the most valuable part of an interview. Finally, when your appointment is scheduled to end, depart—unless the expert invites you to stay.

Many respondents will let you tape-record the interview. However, even if you do record, take brief notes too. Writing things down helps you to concentrate and to remember details later on. As soon as possible after the interview, fill in your notes with details from the tape or from memory.

Professional tip. If you're meeting the expert face to face, dress appropriately. If you wear jeans and a T-shirt to interview the senior partner of a law firm, you may not get past the receptionist.

Interviewing by Mail

Sometimes you will interview an expert by mail rather than in person. Whether you're writing a letter to one person or sending a questionnaire to many people, compose your questions carefully. Remember that you won't be there to explain yourself.

In a letter, keep the number of questions fairly small—usually no more than half a dozen—unless they are the "yes or no" type. Tell the expert when you'd like to receive a reply—allow at least a week, preferably two. And if you don't get an answer, write again.

A questionnaire is helpful when you want to ask many questions of many people. Design it to be clear to the reader and easy for you to compare answers. To achieve this, use questions that involve multiple choice, true or false, or rating an item from 1 to 5. Such formats are easy to fill in, so you'll probably get more replies; they are also easy to tabulate.

Once you have a stack of notes from an interview or the tabulated results from a questionnaire, treat them like notes taken from your reading. Keep track of who said what. Even though your information doesn't come from a book or a magazine, it does come from an outside source; if you don't give proper credit when you write your paper, you will be plagiarizing. Moreover, naming your sources indicates to your readers that you are offering new and valid information, not just rehashing old facts.

Professional tip. Your respondents shouldn't have to pay to answer your questions. So when interviewing by mail, whether by letter or question-naire, always send a stamped, self-addressed envelope. It will greatly in-crease your chance of getting a reply.

EXERCISE 2-5

Look through your college catalog for the names of professors who spe-cialize in the study of the American family. Formulate six questions to ask them that Sar A. Levitan does not answer in the essay on pages 24–26—or that he answers in ways you find hard to accept. (Do *not* conduct an inter-view unless you intend to write a paper. Check with your instructor.)

EXERCISE 2-6

Using the suggestions presented in this section, prepare and conduct an interview with a friend or classmate about his or her area of expertise.

EXERCISE 2-7

Compose a one-page questionnaire asking children about their dessert preferences.

TELEVISION AND RADIO

Television and radio, particularly documentary and news broadcasts, can also be primary sources of information for your writing. But you can't rely on a vague memory of what Dan Rather or Roger Mudd said two months ago; you must take detailed, accurate notes and identify the sources. When writing a paper, check the television listings for programs dealing with your topic; they might be helpful.

Professional tip. Gather as much information about your controlling idea as possible. Don't stop looking when you think you have enough facts to fill the required number of pages. When you have more information than you actually need, you can select the most interesting and effective details and omit the others. And don't ignore information you disagree with. Your writing will be stronger if you can deal with facts that go against your point, not only with those that support it.

SUMMARY

In Step Two—gather information—you should:

- Look for facts and ideas in your own experience.
- Look for facts and ideas by observing the world around you.
- Brainstorm by free-associating a list of information.
- Brainstorm by using the Five W's and H: *Who? What? When? Where? Why?* and *How?*
- Read.
- Interview experts.
- Send out questionnaires.
- Use information from television and radio.

If a man can group his ideas, he is a good writer.

ROBERT LOUIS STEVENSON

Step 3: Organize

Imagine a vacant lot with stacks of cinder blocks, timber, and bricks in one corner, bags of cement and mortar in another, and a big earth mover in the middle. You want to build a house. How do you do it?

One way is to crank up the earth mover and dig a hole in the ground for the foundation. You make it about 20 feet long, 16 feet wide, and 8 feet deep. Then, you mix some cement and pour the basement floor. Tired, you go home.

When you come back the next morning, you begin to wonder, "Is there going to be enough room for the living room, dining room, and kitchen on the first floor, and the two bedrooms and bathrooms on the second? Kitchen! Bathrooms! I forgot to put in the water pipes!" So you tear up the cement floor and start over.

Of course, that isn't the way people build houses. They don't start the actual work until they have laid out a plan on paper, specific down to the last detail. And before building can begin, the plan usually has to be approved by bureaucrats, who make sure that it agrees with the building code.

There is no building code for essays, however, and many writers start their first drafts as soon as they have gathered some ideas and information.

They're not actually doing anything wrong—no roof will fall, no building inspector will shut down construction. But often they are wasting time and effort on a draft that has to be torn up and begun again.

Planning an essay and organizing your information before you write does require some work. But it's much easier to try out different plans in outline form than to write pages and pages and then throw them away. Step Three—organize—offers you some options to use in creating an outline for your writing.

PATTERNS OF DEVELOPMENT

All writing uses patterns. Patterns of letters form words, and patterns of words form sentences. There are paragraph patterns too—there are even patterns for whole essays. These larger patterns are called *patterns of development*. They organize information and ideas so that writing makes sense and is easy to follow.

If you want to explain how to buy a car, for instance, you would organize your information into a *process* pattern, going step by step: "First, borrow money from a rich friend or relative . . . ." Or if you want to write about last Thanksgiving vacation, you would probably organize your information as a *narrative*, starting at the beginning: "I awoke Thursday morning to the screech of a turkey. Or was I dreaming?. . ."

These two patterns grow out of your purpose for writing. But even if a pattern does not emerge naturally, you can choose among several possible patterns in order to achieve your purpose. Suppose you want to write a letter to a newspaper about capital punishment. You might support your point of view by *arguing* that the death penalty has desirable or undesirable effects; by *comparing* societies that have abolished it with those that haven't; by giving *examples* that support your view—a paroled murderer who killed again, an innocent person executed; by *describing* an execution in minute detail; by *defining* the death penalty as "punishment" or as "murder."

A book on capital punishment would probably use all of these patterns. A long paper would probably use several. But in a letter of two or three paragraphs, you might need only one pattern—the one that you feel you can write with most effectively, given your information, your readers, and your purpose.

In the following pages, some often-used patterns of development are presented.

Narration

What it does: Narration reports a sequence of events; it tells a story.

Example:

Whenever I see someone with car trouble parked on the side of the road, I stop and ask if I can help. That's because I remember when I was in the same situation.

I was driving along the highway early one winter evening when sleet started to fall. I turned on the windshield wipers but they didn't work. After a minute or two, the windshield was covered with ice. I could barely see, and I knew I could never make it to the next exit. I pulled to the shoulder of the highway, turned on the flashers, put a handkerchief on the aerial, and waited for someone to help me.

I waited for three hours. The sleet turned to snow. I was freezing and frightened. Finally, a police car stopped and took me to the nearest gas station. I'll never forget the feeling of being rescued—and of waiting to be rescued.

How to use it: Choose the most important events and details, and place them in order. Most often this order will be strictly chronological, beginning with the first event and moving to the last. Sometimes, though, a flashback arrangement is more effective. To emphasize an event later in the story, begin with that event and then return to the rest of the story. Another sequence—the one that is used in the example above—is to begin with an observation in the present that sets the stage for the story that follows. Include dialogue if it helps the narrative, but be sure to keep it natural.

Where to use it: Narration is a useful technique of fiction. But it is also used in essays, news stories, reports, minutes of meetings, history, and autobiographical writing. In addition, anecdotes—brief, entertaining narratives of single incidents—can enrich other patterns.

EXERCISE 3-1

Write a narrative essay based on one of the following topics:

1. a story that makes a point
2. the best joke you have ever heard
3. a childhood memory
4. a sports event you have observed

Description

What it does: Description conveys in words the sights, sounds, tastes, smells, and physical and mental sensations we experience.

Example:

My friend Susan is a walking advertisement for designer clothes. Her powder blue T-shirt is designed by Ralph Lauren, with a Polo insignia decorating the front. The blue jeans she's wearing are neatly pressed and fashionably faded—and display a Calvin Klein label on the back pocket. The low-heeled, brown leather sandals that complete the outfit unfortunately don't have a label. You have to wait until she puts her feet up to see Evan Picone stamped on the soles. Even Susan's perfume is designer created. When I admired the pleasant floral scent, she murmured, "Geoffrey Beene."

How to use it: Choose sensory details that make your subject as tangible and immediate as possible. Arrange them in a logical order. For example, if you are describing a house, you might begin with the outside and end with the inside; you might begin at the bottom and end at the top; or you might take your reader for a walk around it. If you are describing a garden, you might begin with what it looks like, then proceed to its smells and sounds.

Where to use it: Description can be used anywhere to make the abstract concrete and the general specific.

EXERCISE 3-2

Write a description on two of the following topics, making as effective use of sensory details as you can.

1. a sneeze
2. plunging into a swimming pool on a hot day
3. a doctor's office
4. a pineapple
5. taking off in an airplane
6. the world from your window
7. a sunset

Process Instruction and Process Explanation

What it does: Like narration, process instructions and explanations arrange information in chronological order. A process instruction tells the reader how to do or make something. A process explanation tells how something happens.

Examples:

Process Instruction

To get to my house from Main Street, take a number 32 bus west on Elm Street to Crawford Street; it's about a 15-minute ride. Walk south on Crawford Street for three blocks until you reach Fulton Place (*not* Fulton Street, which is one block farther). Turn right on Fulton Place, and walk about half a block to number 179; it's on the right-hand side. Push the button for apartment 5C, and I'll come down and let you in.

Process Explanation

Amending the Constitution of the United States involves several steps. First, a member of Congress must officially propose the amendment. Then, both houses of Congress must approve it by a two-thirds majority, usually after lengthy hearings in their judiciary committees. Finally, three-quarters of the states must ratify the amendment by votes in the state legislatures.

An alternative way to change the Constitution is to convene a constitutional convention. Some policy-makers have discussed this method in recent years, but it has never been used.

How to use it: Divide the process into separate actions or steps. If you're writing process instructions, organize the steps into the sequence that is easiest or safest for your readers to follow. (For example, in this book, "choose a topic" comes first because the other steps depend on it.) Label steps clearly, and describe them in enough detail so that your readers won't be confused. You can further help your readers by numbering the steps or arranging them as a list. If you're writing a process explanation, organize the events chronologically as in a narrative, starting at the beginning.

Where to use it: Process instructions are written for actions as simple as finding your way to a friend's house and as complicated as launching an astronaut into space. A computer program is a process instruction. Process explanations are often used in the natural and social sciences to explain what people, animals, plants, stars, and atoms do.

EXERCISE 3-3

Write a process instruction for one of the following topics, or choose one of your own.

1. how to prepare a favorite recipe
2. how to serve a tennis ball
3. how to pitch a tent
4. how to get from the college library to your writing classroom

EXERCISE 3-4

Write a process explanation for one of the following topics, or choose one of your own.

1. how flowers reproduce
2. how American presidents get nominated
3. how an automobile engine works
4. how the "greenhouse effect" can raise the earth's temperature

Analysis

What it does: Analysis breaks a complex object or idea down into smaller, simpler elements and systematically discusses the elements in order to explain the whole.

Example:

From a distance the painting seems to be a single scene, but closer observation reveals it to be three events, each painted on a separate panel, one blending into the other. On the left is a swimmer poised in the air, midway between the pool's edge and the water. The race is just beginning. The second section depicts a hurdler running a race. He's passed some of the hurdles, but more remain. On the right is a high jumper in the final stage of a jump. His body is arched as he struggles to clear the pole. Thus, with three separate yet unified images, the painter has illustrated the different stages of an athletic competition.

How to use it: Decide which elements you will divide your subject into. If it is an object, break it into its components; if it is an idea, divide it into other ideas. For example, if you plan to discuss a movie, you might begin with a screenplay, then write about the direction, acting, set, cinematography, music, and editing. Each element should be related to the whole, either point by point or in a summary at the end.

Where to use it: Analysis can be used to explain anything large or complex that can be divided into components. It is useful in most kinds of practical writing, from job application letters to scientific reports to personal essays.

EXERCISE 3-5

Write an analysis of one of the following topics:

1. the personality of somebody you know
2. a football team
3. honesty
4. a bicycle
5. a time-sharing computer system

Classification

What it does: Classification is a specialized, formal kind of analysis. It takes a group of similar things (for example, politicians), divides that group into distinct categories on the basis of common characteristics (such as Democrats, Republicans), and then places each member of the group in a category (Edward Kennedy is a Democrat, Howard Baker is a Republican, etc.).

Example:

In the ocean, there's no such fish as a sardine. In the can, though, there are plenty of fish called sardines. There's the Atlantic herring, the Mediterranean pilchard, the Norwegian brisling and sild, and the South African pilchard, to name a few. Since all those are herrings of one sort or another, sardines really turn out to be canned young herrings.

—*Consumer Reports*

How to use it: With your topic and purpose in mind, decide what you want your classification to show. If you are writing about careers, you might want to distinguish between white-collar and blue-collar jobs. If so, you could use this diagram:

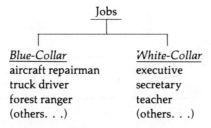

Or you might want to classify jobs according to pay:

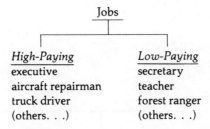

Each category can be subdivided according to your purpose. For example, if you are writing about politicians' views on national health insurance, you could subdivide Democrats and Republicans into conservatives, moderates, and liberals. Or if you are discussing politicians with presidential aspirations, your subdivisions could distinguish between Democrats and Republicans holding office at the national level and at the state and local levels. Classification should always be related to your purpose. If you are writing about what politicians do in their spare time, party affiliation probably doesn't matter; hobbies, sports, and personal interests do.

Charts like those above can present your classification at a glance. But when you have to explain your classification or derive conclusions from it, don't depend on visual aids. Explain it in writing.

Where to use it: Classification breaks down a large, varied mass of information into smaller packages. In practical writing, it can be used in complex writing projects on almost any subject, but it is especially useful in the natural and social sciences and in business.

EXERCISE 3-6

Using diagrams, classify your clothing according to the following categories. Each diagram should include all of your clothing.

1. color
2. material
3. use

EXERCISE 3-7

For one of the following topics (or your own), create a classification and use it in writing a short essay.

1. house pets
2. television shows
3. the college curriculum
4. transportation
5. forms of government

Comparison and Contrast

What they do: Comparison shows the similarities between two or more things, such as people, objects, places, and ideas; contrast shows the differences.

How to use them: Consider the two items you wish to compare and contrast. Make a list of each item's most important and interesting qualities. Those qualities that are similar invite comparison; those that differ invite contrast.

You can organize a comparison or a contrast in two ways:

1. *Block method.* First discuss all the qualities of one item, then all the qualities of the other. Follow the same order in each discussion. The block method is useful when your writing is short and simple, focusing on only a few qualities of the two items.
2. *Point-by-point method.* Discuss one quality at a time for both items. The point-by-point method is useful when your writing is long and

complex, with many qualities of the two items being compared or contrasted.

Examples:

Block Method

The college I attended as an undergraduate was in the middle of a large city. The campus was not really a campus at all, but a few high-rise buildings on noisy city streets. All the classrooms were in one huge tower that rose forty stories out of a fringe of well-trampled lawn, and you traveled from class to class by elevator. Across a busy intersection were the dormitories, three converted apartment buildings around a small concrete courtyard. There were, in fact, other buildings—a modern new library, a chapel, even a stadium—but you had to know the city, or at least the neighborhood, to find them. They were blocks away in different directions along streets clogged with cars and trucks.

Graduate school, in a typical college town, could hardly have offered a sharper contrast. The university was a separate, self-contained world, lying peacefully apart from the town on acres and acres of rolling green lawn. Set among trees and flowering shrubs stood buildings in every architectural style of the past two hundred years—but not one of them more than four stories high. Winding paths crisscrossed the campus, and along the paths were benches. I remember one you could sit on for half a day and the only sounds you'd hear would be the wind in the trees, an occasional airplane, and maybe the distant music of the marching band at practice in the stadium.

Point-by-Point Method

The two houses are similar in many respects, but as you study them room by room you find major differences. For example, the kitchen in the first house has more up-to-date appliances and a good working layout. But the kitchen in the second has room for a table, an advantage for informal eating.

Both houses have large bedrooms and plenty of closet space. But the master bedroom in the first house has a picture window facing a river, whereas the bedrooms in the other house all have small windows that overlook a freeway. The first house has a finished basement, which can be used as a playroom or hobby area. The second has only a small, unfinished basement, which would probably be useful only as a storage space.

Where to use them: Comparison and contrast help to differentiate, give reasons for a choice, emphasize aspects of one item by setting them beside those of another, and explain something unfamiliar by putting it next to something familiar. Comparison and contrast may be used in all kinds of practical writing.

EXERCISE 3-8

Choose one of the following topics, and list the qualities of each of the two items in it.

1. two sports teams, or two individual athletes
2. two countries, cities, or towns
3. George Washington and Abraham Lincoln
4. the place where I grew up and the place where my college is
5. civil disobedience and lawbreaking
6. videocassette systems and videodisk systems

Is block or point-by-point comparison and contrast more effective for your topic? Why? Now choose a second topic, and repeat the exercise.

EXERCISE 3-9

Write a short essay of comparison or contrast based on one of the topics in Exercise 3-8. Or, if you like, create your own topic. Before you begin writing, brainstorm to develop the list of qualities of the two items.

Analogy

What it does: Analogy compares an unfamiliar or abstract concept with something familiar or concrete in order to make the concept easier to understand. Analogy matches up two extremely different things that have something important in common.

Example:

The human body is like an ant colony. In the colony, each ant is created for a specific purpose such as worker, soldier, or queen; each works in perfect coordination with the others for the good of the colony. In the human body, each cell is created for a specific purpose such as circulation or reproduction; each works in perfect coordination with the others for the good of the body.

How to use it: When explaining a difficult concept, try to think of something your readers will understand that in some way resembles your concept. Compare the two, point by point, in your mind (see point-by-point comparisons on page 40). If they match up on all the important points you want to make about the concept, your analogy is true. If they match up on only a few, relatively unimportant points, your analogy is false. For most analogy papers you write, the point-by-point method will be the best way to organize your comparison.

Where to use it: Whenever you are trying to explain an unfamiliar or difficult idea or concept or process, consider using an analogy to help you make your point quickly and effectively. Analogy is often used in popular writing on specialized subjects, notably in the natural and social sciences, and in narratives, descriptions, journalism, and political speeches.

EXERCISE 3-10

Which of the following analogies are true? Which are false? Explain why.

1. Bigotry is like a disease. It can be contained if it is treated immediately. If it is allowed to grow, it can spread to other healthy minds and eventually infect a whole nation. The cure at that stage must be drastic and may be difficult to achieve.
2. Children leaving home are like fledglings leaving the nest. Even though their parents would like them to stay, it's natural to let them go—even to force them out. Like young birds, young people must try their wings. Once they get over their shaky start, they can soar.
3. Love can be compared to a flower. To flourish, it needs care. Kisses are its raindrops, smiles its sunshine, hugs its honeybees.
4. If America is a lumbering elephant, then the OPEC nations are mice. Which frightens the other more?
5. The world is a neighborhood of countries. You try to get along with your neighbors. If they need something, you lend it to them, and if you need something, you borrow it. But tempers can flare. If either neighbor steps over the property line or disturbs the other's life, voices are raised. And if you see a neighbor being robbed or injured, you call the police.

EXERCISE 3-11

Write a short analogy involving one of the following topics:

1. memory
2. the United Nations
3. an individual or team sport
4. how the lungs work
5. a strong personality

Definition

What it does: Definition clarifies general, abstract, or unfamiliar ideas or terms.

How to use it: One way to define a word or concept is to place it into a general class and then differentiate it from other members of the same class. This kind of definition can be stated in a single sentence:

A magnifying glass is a lens that produces an enlarged image of an object.

Democracy is a form of government in which the supreme power is vested in the people.

Another way to define words or concepts is by supplying other more familiar words or phrases with the same meaning. Or define a word by giving its origin.

According to the author, "a synkinetic relationship exists between a dog and its leash." *Synkinesis* is an involuntary movement in one part when another part is moved. It is derived from the Greek words *syn* ("together with") and *kinesis* ("motion").

Sometimes you can define a word by explaining what it does *not* mean. For example:

By *liberty*, I do not mean the freedom to do anything you like. I mean freedom from government and laws arbitrarily imposed without the people's consent.

Abstractions—words that name ideas rather than tangible, material things—almost always have to be defined. In fact, entire books have been written in an effort to define *conservatism, liberalism, truth, relativity,* even the meaning of *meaning.* When writing about an abstraction, try to use a concrete example to relate the idea to the reader's experience. For example:

> What is a *white lie?* A white lie stretches the truth to save someone's feelings. For example, your mother presents you with a T-shirt bearing her picture and asks you whether you like it. You think it's hideous. If you say you like it, you'll be telling a white lie.

Still another way to define a word or concept is to use another pattern of development, such as description (page 33), analogy (pages 40–42), or comparison and contrast (pages 38–40).

Where to use it: Use definition when you need to clarify and emphasize the meanings of words and concepts—especially those that are abstract or that require specialized knowledge your reader may not have.

EXERCISE 3-12

Write a short essay defining one of the following terms:

1. bravery
2. socialism
3. art
4. education
5. success

Illustration (Exemplification)

What it does: Illustration gives substance to a generalization or an abstract idea by providing a series of specific examples.

Example:

> It amazes me that perfectly sane and sober people often go a little bit crazy when naming their children. The mayor of a town in Illinois called himself C. P. Dobbs, and I don't blame him: his parents, in a moment of mineralogical fantasy, had him christened Carborundum Petroleum Dobbs. I found this out from two wonderful little books by John Train called *Remarkable Names of Real People* and *Even More Remarkable Names.* There are dozens of other unfortunates, such as E. Pluribus Eubanks of San Francisco, Ming-Toy Epstein of New York, Pafia Pifia Pefia Pofia Pufia da Costa of Brazil, and Melissy Dalciny Caldony Yankee-Pankee Devil-Take-the-Irishman Garrison of Tryon City, North Carolina.

How to use it: When you write about concepts or ideas, find examples that make your discussions more concrete and easy to understand. Try to support a general statement with pertinent examples that illustrate the generalization and make it more convincing.

Where to use it: Illustration can be used either as the main pattern of development or with other patterns in most college and business writing, including essays, letters, reports, research papers, speeches, public relations writing, recommendations, and analyses. Illustration is especially useful in persuasive writing, when your purpose is to convince the reader that a general statement is true.

EXERCISE 3-13

Write a short essay using at least three specific examples to support or explain one of the following statements:

1. Firstborn children are more likely to be successful than their younger siblings.
2. Isaac Asimov has written books on an astonishing variety of subjects.
3. Sometimes the demands of conscience must be put above the requirements of the law.
4. The best things in life are (or aren't) free.

Visual illustrations are a special kind of example. They can clarify a concept when words alone may be inadequate or confusing—for instance, when you use statistics or when you have to describe precisely how something looks. Visuals include:

1. Pictures: photographs, diagrams, line drawings, sketches, maps, plans
2. Data visuals: charts, tables, graphs (line, bar, and pie)

Whenever you use a visual, place it close to the related discussion, preferably on the same page, and refer to it in your writing. Explain each visual with a caption. Don't use a visual as decoration—it should contribute to clarity. Finally, if you have copied a visual, give credit to the source. (The proper form of credit is shown on page 165.)

Visual illustrations are essential in scientific and technical writing, in journalism, and in any kind of writing that uses complex statistics. For examples of visual illustrations, look through newsmagazines and newspapers.

EXERCISE 3-14

Look through newspapers, magazines, and books, including your text-books. Collect one example of each kind of visual illustration—photograph, line drawing, map, and graph—along with its accompanying text. Would words alone have been sufficient? Did the illustration help clarify the writing? Why or why not?

Cause and Effect

What it does: A cause-and-effect pattern shows a link between events or situations. Unlike narration, which simply reports a series of events, cause and effect tries to establish why events are related. A *cause* may have one or several effects, things it makes happen. An *effect* may have one or several causes, things that make it happen.

How to use it:

1. *Look for causes.* Most things happen for a reason. Often there is more than one cause. In fact, there may be a chain of causes stretching back into the past; unless you include every link in the chain, you can't explain why an effect happened. Or several causes may have worked together at the same time; without one cause, the effect wouldn't have happened at all.

   For example, Ellen might have overslept (*effect*) because she was up late working on a term paper and forgot to set her alarm clock (*cause*). But working late is not just a cause. It is also an effect—something caused Ellen to do it. Perhaps she didn't realize how much time she would need to do the paper and perhaps she had to put off starting it (*effect*) because of a family problem (*ultimate cause*). Of course, the family problem had its own causes, but they add nothing to the explanation of why Ellen overslept. This leads to a good general rule: stop tracing a causal chain when you run out of causes that are directly related to the effect.

   Consider the sinking of the *Titanic*. Over 1500 people died because the ship struck an iceberg; because there were not enough lifeboats aboard to save all the passengers and crew; and because a nearby ship, which might have come to the rescue, had no radio operator on duty to hear the *Titanic's* call for help. All of these events combined to create the disaster. The iceberg was the immediate cause; the ship would not have been damaged without it. However, if any one of the other events had not occurred, many lives would have been saved. This leads to another general rule: include not only the immediate cause of an effect but also the events or conditions that were necessary for the effect to happen.

2. *Look for effects.* Think about a situation or event as a possible cause. What did it make happen? Perhaps nothing, perhaps an effect, or perhaps a cluster or a chain of effects, some significant, some trivial.

For example, suppose the college administration is considering raising tuition. The treasurer believes that one effect of the raise will be to reduce the budget deficit, which has become alarmingly big. The admissions department states that past raises have not made freshman classes any smaller, but have made them more middle-class, less racially mixed, and more dependent on scholarships. The dean of students knows that a tuition raise in the 1960s caused three days of campus demonstrations. However, that has never happened again, and she predicts that it will not happen this time. The dean of faculty, concerned that two distinguished professors have left for better-paying positions at other colleges, wants to raise some salaries to stop the "brain drain"; thus, he supports the tuition raise. Taken all together, these statements, all based on the study of past causes and effects, make it possible for the administration to decide what action to take. The tuition goes up.

Where to use it: Cause and effect can be used in any kind of practical writing—essays, reports, articles—when your purpose is to explain, to investigate, to draw conclusions, to prove or disprove an idea, to accept or reject a course of action. It is particularly useful in the social and natural sciences for explaining present or past events and predicting future occurrences. Because readers often need reasons before they will be persuaded, cause and effect can be especially important in argument (see pages 47–51).

EXERCISE 3-15

Think of each of the following as an effect, and list the causes. For each effect to occur, which would be the immediate cause and which would be necessary conditions or events?

1. the declining birth rate in the United States
2. air pollution
3. renewed interest in fundamentalist religion
4. the high cost of housing in the United States
5. the bombing of Hiroshima and Nagasaki in 1945
6. heart attacks

EXERCISE 3-16

Think of each of the following conditions or events as a cause, and list a probable effect. If other conditions or events would be necessary for the effect to happen, indicate what these would be.

1. Gasoline costs over $2.00 a gallon.
2. Home computers are as cheap and reliable as television.
3. A nuclear bomb is dropped on Washington, D.C.
4. Public transit workers in your home city are on strike.
5. Contact is made with creatures from another world.
6. No loans or scholarships are available for college students.

Argument

What it does: An argument uses evidence and sound reasoning to support a proposition. This proposition—the statement on which an argument is based—is the controlling idea of the argument. In a successful argument, the proposition is so convincingly supported that the reader accepts the writer's conclusion and perhaps acts on it.

How to use it:

1. *Gather evidence.* Evidence is anything—facts, statistics, illustrations, examples—that makes your conclusion easier for your readers to accept. Sometimes, the evidence may be so strong that an argument is a proof—that is, it leaves no possibility for reasonable doubt. For example, an accused murderer must be innocent if he or she was unquestionably in Chicago at the time the murder was committed in Santa Fe. But usually the best you can do is to show that your conclusion fits the facts better than any other.

How much evidence do you need? That depends on what your readers know or believe. Some points are common knowledge—exercise and a well-balanced diet are necessary for good health or employment opportunities for women are better today than they were fifteen years ago—and your readers would be unlikely to disagree. Others are controversial and need more support before your readers will accept them—for example, the causes of the recession in the United States in the early 1980s. But don't indiscriminately scoop up all the facts you can find about your topic. Look for evidence that strongly supports your conclusion—evidence that can be the basis of your argument.

Here are some ways to use evidence:

- *Show your reasoning.* Explain why each piece of evidence supports your conclusion, unless you can be sure your readers will get the point. For example, if you want to argue that *Citizen Kane* is a great movie, define what you mean by movie greatness; give reasons why *Citizen Kane* fits the definition; and support your reasons with facts and examples.
- *Eliminate alternatives.* Even if you cannot prove that your conclusion is true beyond reasonable doubt, you should be able to show that it fits the evidence better than any other. For example, if you want to argue that solar energy is the most promising new source of power, you should not only support that claim but also show that nuclear, wind, and other major sources are less desirable.
- *Show cause and effect.* If you can demonstrate cause and effect, your argument will be particularly strong. For example, drunken driving is statistically the largest cause of fatal car crashes, despite all the laws against it. This is strong evidence that more has to be done to prevent those tens of thousands of needless deaths. If an effect is undesirable, you can attack its cause. But be sensible—banning liquor or cars will solve the problem but cause many others. (For more on cause and effect, see pages 45–47.)
- *Cite similar cases.* If you cannot show cause and effect, try to find evidence of similar situations at other times and places. For example, in arguing against the death penalty, you can point out that the number of murders has not risen in places where the penalty has been dropped (such as in Great Britain and Sweden). Of course, this evidence does not prove anything, or show cause and effect, but it does make it harder for your readers to believe that capital punishment deters murder.

2. *Organize your argument.* The most direct way to present your argument is to begin with your proposition, or controlling idea, and then support it with your evidence. This structure is the easiest for readers to follow, and it is often the best to use. However, if you think your readers are likely to be offended by your conclusion or reluctant to accept your point of view, put it last and lead up to it with your evidence. (See "Order," pages 51–56, for advice on how to sequence your pieces of evidence effectively.)

At some point, you must acknowledge and refute the evidence and arguments that oppose your conclusion or support other conclusions. Where? If you think your own argument is much stronger than the others, state your case first. If the opposing arguments are numerous or strong, however, or if you have some other reason for preferring to put your conclusion after your evidence, you can start by taking on your opponents. Putting your conclusion last will emphasize it.

Where to use it: In practical writing, use argument whenever you want to persuade readers to agree with your position on a particular point and perhaps take a particular action. Also use argument to explain a conclusion that you have reached on the basis of evidence and logical reasoning. Some kinds of writing that often use argument are essays, term papers, exams, proposals, scientific reports, and writing on social and political issues.

EXERCISE 3-17

Write an argument in which you use reasoning and evidence to support one of the following propositions.

1. Movie ratings (G, PG, R, X) should (or should not) be abolished.
2. Grades are a useful (or harmful) way to measure academic achievement.
3. Computers have (or have not) fundamentally changed our everyday lives.
4. Americans should (or should not) make more sacrifices to support our defense and foreign policies.
5. Jogging is (or is not) good for you.

Caution: Some writers try to persuade readers with defective or unethical arguments called *fallacies*. If you can show that an opposing argument is a fallacy, that's a powerful way to rebut it. And if you avoid fallacies in your own writing, your arguments will be stronger. Here are some common fallacies:

- *Circular argument*. Instead of supporting a conclusion with evidence, the writer merely states the conclusion again in different words. For example:

    Everyone should have a fair chance to get a job because there should be equal opportunity in employment.

- *Ignoring the issue*. Instead of sticking to the point, the writer shifts to another that is easier to deal with. For example:

    Environmentalists claim that industries should be forced to install antipollution devices. This is a waste of our resources, because in an industrial society the environment can never be completely pollution-free.

- *Either-Or Fallacy*. The writer tries to make us choose between just two alternatives, even though there are other, often better, possibilities. For example:

    Either we must find more petroleum in the United States or we must rely on nuclear energy.

- *Analogy*. Analogy has its uses in explanation, but it proves nothing in an argument. The fact that two things are alike in some ways can often be misleading, for the similarities may have nothing to do with the conclusion being drawn. For example:

    Crime is a disease of society, and criminals are the germs. We should kill them all.

- *Unjustifiable emotional appeal*. An unjustifiable appeal to the emotions tries to make people decide an issue with their hearts rather than their minds. For example:

    The citizens of Grover Corners have always stood for what is best in the American tradition. They therefore should vote in favor of the school bond.

- *Personal attack*. The writer who commits this fallacy attacks or insults the person being argued against rather than addressing the real issues. For example:

    Senator Mike Cornstarch's bill for relief to the squeegee industry does not merit discussion. He is a traitor to his party and a fool, and he does not deserve to be taken seriously.

EXERCISE 3-18

Some of the following arguments are sound, and some are not. Find the fallacies and identify them by type.

1. Government regulation of industry is bad public policy because it prevents the free working of the marketplace.
2. This country has not seen such political divisiveness since the days of the Civil War. In order to preserve our government and prevent another bloody war, we must outlaw political dissent.
3. Drunken driving is the single greatest cause of traffic accidents. The best way to eliminate drunkenness would be to bring back Prohibition, so unless we are willing to do that we cannot hope to reduce the number of highway fatalities.
4. The choice is clear. Either we must stamp out sexual permissiveness or we must accept the moral decay of our society.
5. I have never suffered from blisters, itching, or rashes from poison ivy, although I know I've touched it many times. I must be immune.
6. Representative Hirshhorn says that unemployment and welfare funds should be increased to support the unemployed victims of the recession. She's a typical knee-jerk liberal so her position should be disregarded.

ORDER

Patterns of development can help you organize your ideas. Some patterns may also help you decide in what *order* to present your information. For example, narration usually begins with the earliest event, then follows the order in which things happened, their chronological order. A process explanation or a process instruction *must* begin with the first step and proceed in sequence from there.

For some topics, however, you may have to select not only a pattern of development but also a particular order to follow. What if you were writing a definition of "courage," for example? Or arguing that course grades are a good (or bad) thing? You would then have many ideas to write about but be unsure what order to put them in. The discussion on pages 56–59 offers some suggestions to help you establish an order when the pattern of development does not dictate one.

Sometimes, regardless of topic or pattern of development, the order in which you present your information is decided for you. For instance, when you applied for admission to college, the forms you filled out organized your answers. When you organize your writing according to a specified *format*, an important part of your writing is done for you.

A scientific report, for example, has a particular arrangement. It usually begins with an abstract, or summary. It continues with four sections, titled "Introduction" (it relates the experiment to previous work), "Materials and Methods," "Results or Observations," and "Discussion."

In business communications, some companies have their own formats. A report might be divided into sections entitled "Problem," "Background," "Analysis," and "Recommendation" or "Comments."

Any organization that receives proposals may require them to be set up in a particular way. Government agencies even print booklets that explain how to organize proposals.

Many magazines and newspapers have their own specific requirements. For example, newspaper stories are usually organized in an "inverted pyramid": the broadest and most striking information comes first, and the more detailed information comes after.

Formats save time and trouble. That's why companies send you form letters. You may even have designed one yourself. Does the following letter seem familiar?

Dear _____ (Aunt Judy and Uncle Stan, Marie and Elton, Laverne. . .),

Thank you so much for _____ (*The Pebble Book*, the calculator, the waterbed. . .). It has been _____ (fascinating reading, useful for my budgeting, a unique nautical experience. . .).

I'm so happy that you helped me celebrate my _____ (wedding, graduation, divorce. . .).

_____ (Love, Fond regards, Yours. . .),
Clarence

EXERCISE 3-19

Find samples of formats in newspapers, magazines, business letters, and your own mail. Are they effective? Why or why not?

Kinds of Order

Although most practical writing doesn't follow a specified format, its order must still be carefully planned. If information is just thrown together, readers will become puzzled, confused, and maybe even angry.

Many reports, essays, and other kinds of practical writing have three parts:

- An *introduction* states the controlling idea and often provides some background for it. If there is no controlling idea—for example, if you are describing a car accident or reporting a baseball game—you should still provide an introduction to explain what you are writing about.
- The *body*, in between the introduction and conclusion, contains the information that explains or supports the controlling idea or otherwise achieves the purpose of the writing. The body is by far the longest part. An introduction or conclusion is often no more than a paragraph, but the body is usually at least several paragraphs long. The body of a piece of writing is thus the most difficult part to organize.
- A *conclusion* restates the controlling idea or sums up the whole. You may not need to round your paper off with a conclusion. If you are describing a process or giving instructions, when you reach the end just stop.

The following sections present three kinds of order you can use to your writing.

CLIMACTIC ORDER

Sequence: Climactic order arranges information by increasing importance, interest, controversy, or complexity.

Example:

I needed the key to get into the house. I looked under the mat where I usually hide it; it wasn't there. Did I put it somewhere else? I looked under the flowerpot, in the mailbox, above the door, in the doghouse. Just when I thought I would have to break a window, I found it—in my pocket.

Effect: First, climactic order keeps your readers reading. Once they realize that the further they read, the bigger the payoff, they will stay with you to the end. Second, information placed at or near the end of a piece of writing may be more memorable for your readers because it is the last thing they read. Third, if your topic is complex or technical, easier material at the beginning will help readers to understand the harder material at the end.

Climactic order is especially useful if your topic is controversial. You may take it for granted that the military draft should not be reinstated, but your readers may strongly disagree. If so, develop your argument with that controversy in mind, and reserve your opinion for last. By waiting until the end, you will have established grounds for your readers to agree with you or at least to see that your opinion is a reasonable one.

You can also use the opposite order, anticlimactic, which arranges writing in decreasing order of importance. If you know that many of your readers are distracted or busy and may stop reading before the end, put the most interesting and important information at the beginning. Most newspaper stories and business letters do this.

EXERCISE 3-20

Write a paragraph on one of the following topics, arranging the facts or points in either climactic or anticlimatic order:

1. the reasons for going to college
2. mandatory jail sentences for drunken drivers
3. an allergic reaction
4. the benefits of having a woman on the Supreme Court

CHRONOLOGICAL ORDER AND FLASHBACK

Sequence: Chronological order usually begins with the earliest event or situation, then reports subsequent events in the order that they happened. Sometimes you can vary chronological order by using a *flashback*—you can begin with the story's ending, then flash back to the beginning.

Examples:

Chronological Order

The mayor entered the room, faced the television cameras, and asked if there were any questions. When no one spoke up he said, "Don't be afraid, I don't bite." A man in the back of the room raised his hand.

"Yes," said the mayor. "The man in the back."

The man stood up and smiled. "I don't have a question," he said. "I just want to be on TV. Hi Mom!"

Flashback

She stood on the podium clutching the gold statuette. When the crowd finished applauding and sat down, she spoke. "Thank you for this award. It is the highlight of my career."

Twenty years before, as a child on a South Carolina farm, she had dreamed of being an actress. When other children were playing with dolls or roller-skating, she would be inventing characters and writing skits. After hours of rehearsal, she would set the dining-room chairs in front of the picture window and pull the curtains closed. Then, with the stage set, she would disappear behind the curtains to make her entrance before her adoring, imaginary audience.

Effect: When the information you are presenting involves events that occur in a time sequence, chronological order is the simplest and most natural way to organize your material. Like climactic order, it also helps build suspense: the reader has to finish in order to find out how the story ends.

Flashback is useful when a story's outcome is more important than the events leading up to it. By beginning with the outcome and then telling how it happened, you give it the desired emphasis.

EXERCISE 3-21

Using chronological order, write a paragraph on one of the following topics:

1. a meeting you have attended
2. your favorite meal
3. a typical day during exam week
4. painting a room

SPATIAL ORDER

Sequence: Spatial order presents the details of a physical description by moving from point to point, such as:

- from left to right, or right to left
- from near to far, or far to near

- from front to back, or back to front
- from top to bottom, or bottom to top

Example:

The typical modern orchestra has at least eighty-five instruments, divided into four sections. Arranged across the front of the orchestra is the string section, which usually includes more than half the instruments. Just behind the strings, the woodwinds are grouped on the left and the brass instruments on the right. Behind them is the percussion section. Although this is a typical arrangement, the position of the instruments can vary depending on the conductor, the composition, and the shape of the stage.

Effect: If, in writing a description, you want to emphasize one physical detail over all the others, you might choose to use climactic order. Often, however, what is most important is how all the details combine to make the whole. When your main concern is to show your reader how details are arranged, use spatial order.

EXERCISE 3-22

Using spatial order, write a paragraph on one of the following topics:

1. a person
2. an amusement park
3. a kitchen
4. a football stadium

COORDINATING YOUR PLAN

As mentioned earlier, to organize your writing you need both a *pattern of development*, which grows out of your purpose for writing, and an *order* in which to put your facts, ideas, and examples.

Which patterns and orders work together best? Usually you will have several options.

If you're writing about cars, your statement of purpose might be, "I want to explain the similarities and differences between American and Japanese compact cars." In this case, your pattern of development has to be comparison ("similarities") and contrast ("differences"). There are many points on which to compare American and Japanese cars, so you decide to use point-by-point rather than block comparison. What order should you use?

You can use spatial order—you might begin with the outside of the car and move to the inside:

body styling
available colors
length, width, height
number of doors
interior decoration
passenger space
space for luggage
dashboard, steering wheel, and gear shift
type of motor
electrical system
cooling system

You can use chronological order:

purchasing cost
performance and mileage
maintenance
longevity
trade-in value

You can use climactic order—you might begin with the features you consider to be least important and build up to those you consider most important:

appearance
reliability
mileage
performance
cost
safety

Look again at the three lists just presented. Each has a different effect on readers. The spatial order seems almost scientific; it focuses on what can be observed about a car. Chronological order focuses on what the reader would experience as a car buyer and owner. Climactic order focuses on the features that would influence the reader's decision to buy one car or another.

The choice is yours. Depending on your purpose for writing, each of the orders can be effective. And once you have chosen, it will be easy to write an outline for your paper.

The following list shows the orders that are most natural and useful with each pattern of development.

Pattern	Order
Narration	Chronological
Description	Spatial Climactic
Process	Chronological
Analysis	Climactic Spatial
Classification	Climactic
Comparison and contrast	Chronological Spatial Climactic
Definition	Climactic
Illustration	Chronological Spatial Climactic
Analogy	Climactic
Cause and effect	Chronological Climactic
Argument	Chronological Climactic

EXERCISE 3-23

For each of the following statements of purpose, choose an appropriate pattern of development and a suitable order.

1. I want to report on the president's recent press conference.
2. I want to tell a story about the kindest person I ever met.

3. I want to show how to develop self-confidence.
4. I want to persuade people that taxes should be raised again to support needed social programs.
5. I want to explain the continuing problems of Native Americans living on reservations.
6. I want to compare cross-country skiing with downhill skiing.
7. I want to show why Germany was receptive to the Nazi party.

WRITING AN OUTLINE

An artist often makes a preliminary sketch of a painting before adding detail or color. And professionals in all fields understand the importance of a blueprint or game plan in order to avoid costly mistakes.

At this point you have decided what to write about, analyzed your audience, and stated your purpose and controlling idea (Step One); you have gathered information (Step Two); and you have decided on a pattern of development and an order as a means of organization (Step Three). To convert all this into an outline, you arrange your information and ideas according to pattern and order.

Informal Outline

Practical writing is sometimes short and simple: a note to a friend, a brief essay, an answer to a test question, a memo. Maybe you have only a small amount of information to convey and a simple statement of purpose: "I want to explain why I was absent from class last week." If so, perhaps you can do without an outline. Just review your information and mentally arrange the necessary details into the pattern and order you choose.

Most writing, however, benefits from the writer's arranging major facts or ideas into the best order and jotting them down. This informal outline is sometimes called a "scratch outline" or a "rough outline," because it doesn't have to be neat—it won't be seen or judged by others. Your only concern is to get the best ideas down in the order you've chosen.

Informal outlines don't have to be detailed. Concentrate on the major ideas or facts that most directly support your statement of purpose and controlling idea and therefore might serve as topics for the individual paragraphs of your writing. Include only as much detail as you need to be certain that you have adequate information to develop each major idea or fact. The following guidelines will help you write effective informal outlines.

1. *Select your major ideas.* You may have done this to some extent as you gathered information in Step Two. If not, choose the major ideas from your brainstorming list. If you're working with note cards, classify them into related groups under major headings. Select only ideas that focus on your statement of purpose.

2. *List the major ideas in the best possible sequence according to the pattern and order you've chosen.* If your major ideas are written on paper, you can rearrange them simply by numbering and renumbering them until they're in the order that seems best.

   As you move your ideas around, some may turn out to be not major ideas but rather supporting information for major ideas. Make these supporting ideas subentries under the major ideas in your outline.

   Don't be afraid to arrange and write several versions of an outline in order to achieve the best possible organization. Arrows, cross-outs, and additions are signs of thinking.

   If you're working with note cards, take advantage of their flexibility. Shuffle them around on a table or pin them on a bulletin board until you find the order that suits you best.

3. *Check your outline.*
   - Are all of the ideas related to your statement of purpose and controlling idea?
   - Does the outline follow your chosen pattern and order?
   - Are there sufficient ideas or facts to support each major point in the outline?

Let's assume your topic is vegetarianism. Your statement of purpose is:

I want to persuade readers to switch to vegetarian diets.

And your controlling idea is:

The advantages of vegetarian diets far outweigh the disadvantages.

The pattern of development that seems most appropriate is classification; you are going to subdivide the consequences of vegetarianism into two categories—advantages and disadvantages—and list them accordingly.

Look back at the sample brainstorming list on pages 19–22. In that example, it was assumed that you wrote down whatever fact or idea came into your head about this topic. Now, as you outline, your goal is to put the best points from that list in the best order.

As you go through your information, continue to cross out, change, narrow, and broaden. Put small ideas under bigger ones. Outlining tells you if you're not going anywhere or if you need more information. You may need to do several versions of your outline before you're satisfied.

Are there any points listed under advantages of vegetarian diets that you don't need? Any you should add? Any that can be combined? "Less fat" and "less cholesterol" seem to go together. "You won't get trichinosis" seems a small point; perhaps it can be dropped. "Fuel conservation" and "water conservation" can be grouped together with "grazing animals can harm the environment" under a new major idea, "less damage to the environment."

Apply the same process to your list of disadvantages of vegetarian diets. Then check your informal outline to be sure you're satisfied with it. You may find as you outline that your information does not support your controlling idea; that is, you discover that you now think the disadvantages of vegetarian diets outweigh the advantages. If so, you do not have to abandon your topic and begin your paper from scratch. Instead, you may decide that your purpose should be to convince your readers *not* to become vegetarians. It is a simple matter at this point to change your controlling idea, for example:

> A vegetarian diet offers many advantages, but the disadvantages outweigh them.

That's what is so useful about outlining. It enables you to assess your information. It helps you to think.

You might end up with an informal outline that looks like this:

Vegetarian Diets: Advantages and Disadvantages

Advantages
   Less fat and cholesterol
      —less chance of heart disease
   Fewer chemicals needed to preserve vegetables
      —fewer cancerous agents
   Fresher
      —can grow own food
   Less damage to the environment
      —conserves fuel and water
      —less water pollution
      —grazing animals can harm the environment

You don't kill animals
Less expensive

Disadvantages
Protein and other vitamin deficiencies
—may need vitamin supplements
—tend to get anemia
Diet not as varied
—complex combination of recipes needed
—lack of textures, tastes
Hard to adhere to in a meat-eating society
—looked upon as a cultist
—tend to get self-righteous

EXERCISE 3-24

Following are four groups of notes based on the topic of choosing a major in college. Supply a statement of purpose and, if possible, a controlling idea for each group of notes. Then decide on a pattern and an order for each, and organize the notes as an informal outline.

1. Arts and Sciences
      —arts, literature, and humanities
      —social sciences
      —biological sciences
   Occupational
      —engineering
      —business
   Physical Sciences

2. Political Science and Sociology
      —subject matter
      —job prospects
      —salary
      —social usefulness
      —scholarship availability

3. I can't stay in college without a scholarship.
   My cousin was a nurse and seemed to like her job.
   There are plenty of nursing jobs.

I was always interested in health care.
There are scholarships available for nursing.

4. Narrow down choices; weigh benefits and disadvantages of each.
Make a decision
Search out available majors
   —Liberal arts vs. occupational
Do mechanics
   —Register choice of major
   —Meet with curricular adviser for that major
Know thyself
   —Interests
   —Aptitudes
   —Past experience
Get help
Tests for aptitudes, interests
Counseling center
Talk to instructors
Role models, friends

Formal Outline

When your writing is complex, or important, or to be graded, you may decide to construct a more detailed, formal outline. A formal outline is more structured than an informal one and more difficult to write. But with complex ideas, a formal outline is worth the effort, because it will guide and simplify your writing.

Just as in an informal outline, you'll write down your statement of purpose, be aware of your pattern, select your main ideas, sort and list your main ideas in the order you choose, and check the outline. But now you'll be working with greater complexity. Your ideas and facts will often come from note cards. You will subdivide your main ideas into minor categories. In addition, you must:

- *Establish all major ideas before minor ideas.* After you've identified and outlined the broad, major ideas, study your notes for minor ideas within each major area. Complete the outline section (I,A,1,a. . .) for one major area before starting the next. This lets you be sure each section is complete and well balanced.

- *Be consistent.* Whatever symbols, indentation, or construction you choose, be clear and consistent. These mechanics are signposts that quickly tell you the relationships between the parts of the outline. Headings should be parallel. Each major idea should be equal in value, and each minor idea should be equal in value.
- *Be complete.* Be sure that you've put down all the details, examples, and subordinate points that you plan to include in your paper. You will be depending on the outline as you write, so don't leave out any significant idea or fact.

There are two types of formal outlines, *topic outlines* and *sentence outlines.* Topic outlines use words or phrases as headings. When you are concerned with facts more than ideas, the topic outline is convenient. For example:

History of Still Photography

I.   Early Experiments
   A.   Early failures
      1.   Joseph-Nicéphore Niépce (France)
      2.   Thomas Wedgwood (England)
   B.   Important early breakthroughs
      1.   Louis-Jacques-Mandé Daguerre and the daguerreotype (France)
      2.   William Henry Fox Talbot and the negative-positive system (England)
      3.   Frederick Scott Archer and negatives on glass (England)
II. Modern Advances
   A.   Richard Leach Maddox—gelatin bromide emulsion for shorter exposures
   B.   George Eastman—Kodak camera for amateurs
   C.   Color photography
      1.   1907—autochrome process
      2.   1935—Kodachrome process, invented by Leopold Mannes and Leopold Godowsky
   D.   One-step photography—Edwin Land and the Polaroid camera

Sentence outlines use complete sentences as headings. Often, with little or no change, these sentences can be incorporated in the first draft of your writing. Although it requires more work at this stage, a sentence outline will save you time later. Here is an example of a sentence outline:

American Government:
Representative Democracy vs. Oligarchy

I. Historically there are four basic forms of government.
   A. A *dictatorship* places control in a single person.
   B. An *oligarchy* places control in a relatively small group of people.
   C. A *direct democracy* gives each citizen's preference equal weight on all major issues.
   D. A *representative democracy* allows groups of citizens, usually from the same geographic region, to select representatives.
II. Although the United States officially has a representative democracy, it really looks more like an oligarchy.
   A. In a country this large, it is difficult for a representative form of government to work well.
   B. Certain political participants have more power than others.
      1. Sociologist C. Wright Mills first popularized the concern about a "power elite" in American government.
      2. Several scholarly studies confirm the existence of a controlling group in American life.
         a. Power in contemporary society is often centered in large corporations.
         b. Freitag, Mintz, and Domhoff have documented the interchange of personnel between major corporations and the federal government.

Your outline will guide you in the next step of the writing process. If you take the time to organize carefully now, you will be able to enjoy Step Four—write a draft.

EXERCISE 3-25

What is wrong with the following formal outline? Identify as many problems as you can, and rewrite the outline to correct them.

How to Lose Weight

I. Improve your eating habits.
   A. Eat less fattening foods.
      1. fruits and vegetables
      2. fish and lean meats
      3. You should eat smaller quantities.
   B. Exercise
      1. briskly
      2. frequently
         a. Exercise for at least a half hour, three times a week.

EXERCISE 3-26

Using Steps One through Three, prepare to write a paper on a topic of your choice. Include a formal outline.

SUMMARY

In Step Three—organize—you should:

- Choose a pattern of development: narration, description, process, analysis, classification, comparison and contrast, analogy, definition, illustration, cause and effect, or argument.
- Decide which order to arrange your information in: climactic (or anti-climactic), chronological (or flashback), or spatial.
- Write an outline arranging your information according to your chosen pattern of development and order.

Phase Two: Freewriting

Freewriting. The term suggests a ballpoint pen gliding over reams of shiny paper. Free! That's a good way to feel during Step Four—write a draft.

In freewriting, you don't have to worry about details such as subject-verb agreement, or how to spell *resuscitate*, or even whether you've got all the dates and places right. You alone will read—and judge—your draft. You can correct any mistakes later, when you rewrite.

Some people get tense and anxious when they start to put words on paper. They think, "I don't have time to write a rough draft. I'd better make the first one count." For them, writing becomes frustrating and time-consuming as they fret over words and phrases. And the result still needs to be revised. This experience often causes writer's block, the inability to write at all. Freewriting eliminates this problem. Believe it or not, writing a draft can be the most enjoyable part of writing.

The idea is to get the pencil moving quickly.

BERNARD MALAMUD

Step 4: Write a Draft

Unless you are writing something very short or very informal, you should write a rough draft before you tackle a final copy. This rough draft may be your only draft, or it may be the first of several. But no matter how many drafts you write, for each you should warm up, let loose, and cool down.

WARM UP

Smart runners know they need the right shoes, the right surface, and the right stretching exercises. Writers also need the right equipment, the right environment, and the right preparation to ease the way ahead.

Equipment

Equipment should be in working order and within reach. It should include:

erasers	paper clips	scissors
extra typewriter ribbon	pencils	tape or paste
note cards	pencil sharpener	typewriter
paper	pens	

A good dictionary and a handbook of English grammar and usage are essential. Other useful aids include a style manual, an atlas, an almanac, an encyclopedia, and a thesaurus.

Environment

Environment will greatly affect your writing, so try to create a special area where you can keep and use your writing equipment. Find a library carrel, an unused room, or just a quiet corner away from the stereo and television.

Ask those around you not to bother you while you're writing. It usually helps. So does a closed door with a "Do not disturb" sign. And if you can take the phone off the hook, do it.

Other elements that improve the writing environment include:

- A *comfortable chair* with good back support.
- *Good lighting*. Avoid glare; facing a window can cause eyestrain and distractions.
- *Moderate temperature*. When your fingers are turning blue or you're perspiring on the paper, the temperature is not moderate.
- *Rewards*. Drinks and snacks can ease anxiety and save potentially distracting trips away from writing.

Preparation

Preparation can help you avoid some of the common writing traps.

Schedule a regular writing time. The most productive professional writers usually force themselves to observe more or less regular "office hours" for their writing because they know that writing takes discipline. When you have a writing project, don't wait until the night before your paper is due. Instead, try to reserve adequate time every day at the same time. If you're a morning person, you could write with the sunrise; if you're a night person, you could write instead of watching reruns of *M*A*S*H*. But be realistic. Most writers can't concentrate for more than about three hours at a sitting.

Set writing goals. Use your writing time wisely. Setting a tangible goal—paragraphs, pages, or sections—helps you to produce. For example, if you're writing a short theme, try to finish a draft in one sitting. For longer projects, break the writing into logical sections—pages, units, or chapters. If you're writing about Six Famous Women in Eighteenth-Century America, set a realistic goal, such as one of the six each day.

Prime yourself. Look at your brainstorming list, go over your notes, review your outline. Have all your information handy for reference.

Relax. If it helps, bend into a lotus position or take a bicycle ride before sitting down to write. Moreover, to write your best, you should be rested. Writing, like most things, suffers when you're tired. (If you've scheduled your writing wisely, however, you shouldn't lose any sleep over it.)

You should feel ready and eager to write. You've chosen your topic and gathered and organized your information—now it's time to get the words down.

LET LOOSE

The rough draft doesn't have to be good writing, and even for professional writers, it often isn't. As you freewrite, you should concentrate on *what* you're writing rather than on how you're writing: on ideas and the relationships between ideas rather than on grammar, spelling, and punctuation. Of course, correct usage is preferable—but you don't have to be overly concerned with it at this step in the writing process. There will be plenty of time to take care of these matters in Step Six. So relax. Following are a few practical suggestions to help you write your draft.

Use only one side of the paper. If you write on both sides, later on you'll have difficulty reorganizing your work and moving sections around.

Number each page. It prevents confusion later as your pages increase. (If you have many sections, number the pages temporarily 1-1,1-2, etc., or A-1, A-2, etc., so that both unit and page numbers are clear.)

Try typing the rough draft. Typed copy solves the problem of illegible handwriting. And even if you type slowly, you'll often be able to transfer your thoughts to paper more quickly than if you write them by hand. For long papers, it may be less tiring too.

Some writers who write by hand favor a pen because it's easy to read—it doesn't smudge like penciled copy. Yet others prefer to use pencil because they can easily correct and erase mistakes later on. Whichever you select, write as legibly as you can.

Double- or triple-space your writing, whether you type or handwrite, and leave plenty of margin space on all sides of the paper so that you can fit in revisions later.

Write steadily. Try to keep your thoughts flowing and don't stop unnecessarily. Once you've established a writing rhythm, any break of more than a few seconds can disrupt your thought process and disturb the smooth, steady rhythm of your writing. Sometimes, you may have to stop and read what you've just written in order to check your direction. And you may have to look back at your notes. If that happens, don't worry. Just resume your steady pace as soon as you can.

Don't confuse writing steadily with writing quickly. Set a comfortable pace, not an indoor record. If speed alone is your goal, it can lead to something like this:

> Oh boy, here I go. Look how fast I can write without stopping. I'm not self-conscious about it, oh no. Why, I may even look at my outline in the next sentence or two to see what I'm writing about. I can't get over how fast I can write. It's like speedreading only I create the reading myself. Wow! On and on I go, which reminds me of the time. . . .

Leave blanks. If you can't think of the right word, don't stop too long to ponder. Just leave a space or write a note to yourself in brackets, and keep going.

> Jimmy Carter was a . . . [*will find the words*] . . . president.

And rather than disrupt your writing by checking a hard-to-find fact, leave room for it. Then, when you revise, look up the fact and insert it.

> According to Jones, the percentage of American-made automobiles compared to foreign-made sold in the United States will be . . . [*see his book*] . . . in 1990.

What if you have a new idea while writing the rough draft? Put it in. If the idea applies to a section you've already drafted, don't go back and insert it; just make a quick note of the idea—and the page number of the draft where it belongs—for use when you revise. If it applies to a section you haven't reached, make a note keying it to the exact part of the outline where it belongs—for example, II.C.1.

Leave major corrections for later, when you rewrite. If you're the type who can't walk past a crooked picture without straightening it, you will find this difficult. Remember, you're the writer, not the critic; get the words and ideas down, and don't dwell on mistakes.

Don't copy long quotations and footnotes in a rough draft. Instead, leave the approximate space they'll occupy, put the material aside for later reference, and keep writing. Add them when you revise.

- *Be flexible.* Despite your efforts, the writing of your draft won't always go the way you planned.
- *If you run out of time* before meeting your writing goal, try to find out why. Did you write steadily? Did you waste time? Did you set too high a goal? The answers can help you next time.
- *If you finish early,* check whether you covered all the topics in your outline and all the information in your notes. Did you just allow more time than was necessary? The more you write, the easier it will be to predict your writing pace.
- *If you're not producing,* and your head keeps hitting the desk, don't force yourself to keep going. Stop and try to add some time later in the day, or the next day, when you're refreshed.
- *If you're uninspired* or just can't get going, try starting somewhere besides the beginning. Some writers always start with the section they're most familiar with or that they find most enjoyable. (This advice is especially helpful on essay exams. You can go back to the problem area later.)
- *If you feel inspired,* whether it's during your scheduled writing time or at 3 A.M., make the most of it. Don't go back to sleep assuming you will remember that perfect phrase when you wake up. Inspiration is rare and fleeting.

Professional tip. Because you will revise and recopy later, you can write a draft on the backs of used sheets of paper. Not only will this remind you that the draft is rough; it will recycle the paper.

EXERCISE 4-1

Use one of the following topics to work through Steps One through Three—choose a topic, gather information, organize. Then freewrite a rough draft for at least fifteen minutes.

1. the qualities I expect in a friend
2. marijuana should (not) be legalized
3. my dream house (job, weekend, etc.)
4. why gun control is (not) a good idea

5. how I feel about dogs (cats, squirrels, etc.)
6. why _____ is my favorite sport
7. a comparison of music of the 1970s with music of the 1980s

---

COOL DOWN

When you've finished your writing, put it away and do something else. Now is the time to reward yourself for being so diligent. Take a break: read that escapist novel; eat a chocolate-dipped banana; jump in a hot tub. You need to recharge before rewriting. If possible, wait at least a day. You'll be more objective.

SUMMARY

In Step Four—write a draft—you should:

- Gather your writing equipment in the place you work best.
- Schedule your writing time and set writing goals.
- Prime yourself by rereading your notes and outlines.
- Write steadily, without pausing to correct, until you reach your writing goal.
- Take a break before going on to Step Five.

Phase Three: Rewriting

In the prewriting phase, you were primarily a thinker. In the freewriting phase, you were a writer. Now, in the rewriting phase, you will become a critic.

Rewriting may be the most important step of all. As Mario Puzo, author of *The Godfather*, stated, "Rewriting is the whole key to writing." That's why the economist John Kenneth Galbraith revised his autobiography six times and Ernest Hemingway rewrote the ending to *A Farewell to Arms* thirty-nine times. Every part of the book you're reading now has gone through the typewriter at least five times.

Nearly everything you write deserves to go through the rewriting process at least once. And if a piece of writing is especially important—if your grade, or job, or reputation depends on it—you should rewrite it until you can't make it any better.

After writing the rough draft, you set it aside to let the excitement (or desperation) of getting your words on paper pass. Now get ready to start work again; assemble your writing equipment in your favorite working place, schedule your working time, and put distractions aside.

Just like prewriting, rewriting has three steps:

Step Five: Revise.
Step Six: Refine.
Step Seven: Recopy.

The steps are separated for your convenience in studying the writing process, but as you write you may often combine the first two.

Sometimes I write essays half a dozen times before I get them into the proper shape.

T. H. HUXLEY

Step 5: Revise

Revising is improving. You change, rearrange, remove from, and add to your rough draft. You should take the draft through Step Five at least once to check how well you've handled content, organization, and paragraphs. If your writing is complex or particularly important, or if you have made extensive revisions, you may have to go through it more than once to make sure you're satisfied. Later, in Step Six, you'll concentrate on improving details, such as word choice, sentence variety, and mistakes in grammar.

First, read through the entire draft to get an overall impression. Use the checklists included in this step to help you identify and correct problems. When you find one, mark it—you can circle it, underline it, or write a quick note in the margin—but don't lose your momentum. Then go through the draft again, this time stopping to correct the problems one by one.

Don't rush. Leave enough time so that you can go slowly. Avoid distractions like listening to the television; you may overlook a glaring error if you're trying to listen to Johnny Carson's monologue while you revise.

To help yourself concentrate, try reading the draft aloud. It will help call attention to any problems that might exist.

MARK UP THE DRAFT

Now is the time to use those margins you left around your draft. Whenever you find something you aren't satisfied with, write a note in the margin. For example:

add more info	put in chron order
clarify	something missing
drop this	wordy
check this (possible	weak argument
factual error)	?

Some of these notes tell you what to do, while others only identify the problems that still have to be solved. For now, you only have to be concerned with spotting the problems.

As mentioned, you'll be looking for misspelled words and grammatical errors in Step Six. Should you pass them by in Step Five? No and yes. No, you shouldn't stop to fix each little detail during this step—the corrections could involve rewriting whole paragraphs, even pages. Do mark the errors though, so you can find them again later: circle misspelled words or incorrect punctuation; put a check or vertical line in the margin next to unclear sentences.

TIPS FOR REVISING

Before you begin, make a photocopy of your draft to mark up. At the end of Step Six, you can neatly transfer the changes to the original, which will make Step Seven, recopying, easier to do.

Use a colored pencil for marking. Your notes, circles, and check marks will stand out when you go through the draft to make revisions. (Some writers use a different colored pencil for each pass through the draft—blue the first time, red the second, and so on—so they can keep track of their progress and focus on their most recent changes.)

Put new material on a separate page, and place it following the page where it belongs. Don't try to cram additions into the margins or to write them on the backs of pages where you might overlook them. Indicate where the new material goes. For example, two inserts for page 12 would be numbered 12A and 12B; you would write "Insert 12A" and "Insert 12B" at the appropriate places on page 12.

If you have numerous inserts, however, or if you have to move several paragraphs around, *cut and paste*. That is, cut the draft into sections; put the sections into the order you want; then paste or tape the pages back together. Your draft can then be read straight through, and you'll be able to tell whether your changes were a good idea.

USE A CHECKLIST

Experienced writers develop a critical eye; problem spots jump off the page at them. But if you have trouble finding the reasons why your writing doesn't work, a checklist can help. Using a checklist can assure you that every aspect of your writing is acceptable.

Following is a checklist for revising. It begins with the most general areas of concern and ends with the most specific.

A Checklist for Revising

Content (refer to your outline and notes)
- ✔ Does the draft include all the ideas in the outline?
- ✔ Does the draft include all the important material you gathered during prewriting?
- ✔ Does every fact, idea, and argument in the draft relate to your statement of purpose and controlling idea?
- ✔ Have you supplied enough facts and details to support each point?
- ✔ Are your facts, figures, and quotations accurate?

Organization (refer to your outline)
- ✔ Does the draft follow the order of the outline?
- ✔ Are your chosen patterns of development and order effective?

Paragraphs
- ✔ Is each paragraph unified?
- ✔ Is each paragraph well developed?
- ✔ Is each paragraph coherent?

Opening, Ending, Title
- ✔ Does the draft have an effective opening?
- ✔ Does the draft have an effective ending?
- ✔ Does the draft have a good title?

If your writing is short and simple, you may be able to keep all areas of the checklist in mind as you read your draft. Often, though, you'll use one part of the checklist at a time, such as the first one, Content. You'll read through the draft to judge its content before going on to the next part of the checklist, Organization.

The following pages examine the checklist item by item and offer suggestions for revising your draft.

CONTENT

As you read your draft, make sure you didn't leave out any of the information or ideas you gathered in Step Two. Moreover, determine whether you need additional information to make your writing more convincing and effective or whether some of the facts and ideas you have included should be cut because they don't fit your purpose and controlling idea. Finally, check your facts, figures, and quotations to make sure they are accurate.

✓ **Does the draft include all the ideas in the outline?**
If not:
Freewrite to fill in the gaps, and insert the new material where it's needed. Sometimes, however, an omitted point *should* be left out. For example, suppose your draft starts with your *second* point, leaving out the first. If you are using climactic order, the first point is the least important; if you have plenty of other points, leaving out the weakest may make your writing stronger. But don't make this decision just to save yourself some work. Unless the omission is an improvement, fill the gap.

✓ **Does the draft include all the important material you gathered during prewriting?**
If not:
Freewrite new sentences or paragraphs, adding the omitted information.

✓ **Does every fact, idea, and argument in the draft relate to your statement of purpose and controlling idea?**
If not:
Cut out all irrelevant material, or adapt your controlling idea to fit your information. If some information in the draft doesn't directly relate to your controlling idea, it may just be a digression—a detour from your main line of thought. Before you cross it out, though, look at it carefully; perhaps it's trying to tell you something. Unconsciously, you may have been writing about a different controlling idea, one you found more interesting or convincing. For example, you may have intended to write about excessive vio-

lence on television, but while freewriting digressed to the subject of how television viewing in general influences children's behavior. If you really want to write about the effects of television on children, change your controlling idea. (Remember that if you do, you may have to gather more information, rethink your plan of organization, and write another draft.) Otherwise, cut out the digression and get back on course.

When you have no controlling idea, make sure your writing follows the statement of purpose. For example, if your purpose is to explain how a caterpillar becomes a butterfly, anything you included in your draft about butterfly collectors would be a digression and should be cut.

✓ **Have you supplied enough facts and details to support your points?**
If not:
Support your generalizations with specific facts and examples. Your readers need to be shown plenty of supporting facts, details, and evidence not only to understand fully what you are writing about, but also to believe that you've done a responsible job.

Make sure you have supplied every step in a process instruction or explanation.

Flesh out your narrative and descriptions with lots of specific detail.

Narrow your controlling idea or statement of purpose to fit your information. If you absolutely can't brainstorm any more information or find what you need in outside sources, narrow the scope of your paper so that the information you do have is sufficient. For example, if your original controlling idea was "Southern cities are experiencing a renaissance," but most of your information is about Atlanta, you should probably change your controlling idea to something like "Atlanta epitomizes the vigorous growth that is occurring in cities throughout the South." If necessary, go back to Steps Three and Four to organize and freewrite a new draft.

✓ **Are your facts, figures, and quotations accurate?**
If not:
Look up all questionable information in reliable sources. Use your own books if you can, but be prepared to go to the library. If you're citing statistics, you must have sources to back them up. Readers will probably take your word for it if you write, "The U.S. Department of Labor announced in 1982 that one-fifth of American workers belong to labor unions." But if you write, "One-fifth of American workers belong to labor unions," many readers will wonder how you know that. Check all dates. And always check quotations.

Modify absolute statements and terms. If you are sure that a piece of information is reasonably accurate, but you can't locate its source, you don't have to throw it out; just be honest with your readers. For example, instead of writing, "One-fifth of American workers belong to labor unions," write "I read recently that about one-fifth of American workers belong to labor unions." If you can't check the exact wording of a quotation, use indirect quotation rather than quotation marks.

Check the draft against your notes to catch copying errors. Some information is very easy to miscopy—especially numbers, dates, names, and foreign words. The French expression *esprit de corps* can come out *espirit de corpse. Tuesday* can wind up *Thursday,* and *August 7* can become *August 17.* So be careful to check against notes.

Don't mistake opinions for facts. An opinion is not fact. It may be a conclusion based on facts, or it may be a prejudice that pays no attention to facts or even denies them. It is a fact that Warren G. Harding was president from 1921 to 1923; nobody can disagree with that. Whether he was a capable president, or an intelligent and honest man, are matters of opinion on which people may reasonably disagree. Whenever you use an opinion, then, identify it as such and indicate whether the facts support it. For example:

> Many historians say that Warren G. Harding was one of America's worst presidents. Under his nose, members of his administration embezzled public funds and sold favors for bribes, and millions of dollars found their way into the wrong pockets during a period of less than three years. Ultimately, high officials in three different government departments were sentenced to prison, and two others committed suicide when exposed.

The first sentence states an opinion and says who holds it. The rest of the paragraph supplies some of the facts on which that opinion is based—not all of the facts, but enough to support the opinion.

ORGANIZATION

As you revise, you may have a vague feeling that something is wrong with the writing. An idea seems out of place, a paragraph doesn't seem to relate to the one before it, or the whole draft seems to fade out at the end. These are all organizational problems.

Of course, you planned your organization in Step Three. You chose a pattern of development, decided on an order for your information, and wrote an outline that you meant your draft to follow. However, when free-writing the draft, you may have drifted away from your outline, started putting things in a different order, added some new material, or forgot to include something important from your notes. Or perhaps you followed your plan, but now that it's fleshed out in writing it doesn't seem to work. You can find out what's wrong and fix it.

🗸 **Does the draft follow the order and content of your outline?**
  If not:
Cut and paste to rearrange the parts of the draft so that they follow your intended order. Of course, before you cut your draft apart, you should be sure that the fault lies in the draft and not in the outline. It's always possible that the outline itself needs revision.

Freewrite sentences or paragraphs based on any part of the outline that you accidentally left out of the draft. Insert them where they belong.

Look critically at any new information, ideas, or arguments you included in your draft that weren't in the outline. If the additions strengthen your writing, decide on the best place for them, and move them there. Suppose you are writing an argument against smoking. Your outline gives four supporting reasons: it's expensive, stale smoke smells bad, being a slave to such a habit is degrading, and smoking kills you. The reasons are arranged in climactic order. When you are almost finished with the draft, however, you think of another reason—there are many places where smoking is banned—and you immediately write it down. Later, as you are revising your draft, you realize that, by adding this point after your point about death, you are creating an anticlimax. So you place the new point earlier in the draft, and you revise the outline accordingly.

Look critically at any section of the draft that departs from the outline in pattern of development or order. Decide whether the approach of the outline or the approach of the draft more effectively achieves your purpose, and revise accordingly. Suppose you had planned to explain the generation gap between you and your parents through a series of comparisons and contrasts. After two paragraphs, however, you took off in another direction and narrated some stories as examples of the gap. If you like this approach better, do this:

1. Draw up a quick, informal outline for your new plan of organization. (You may have to decide on a different order—chronological, for example, or climactic.)

2. Rearrange the draft so that it follows your new outline.
3. If necessary, freewrite a new beginning to fit the new approach.

If the new approach seems less effective than the one you originally planned to use, go back to your old outline and start freewriting again at the point where you stopped using comparison and contrast.

✔ Are your chosen patterns of development and order effective?
If not:
Look for defects in your pattern of development.

- *Narration.* Does your narration present the events exactly as they occurred? If you have omitted events or given them out of chronological sequence, is it effective, or is it part of the problem?
- *Description.* Have you included enough specific details—sights, sounds, sensations—so that your readers can envision the person, object, or scene you describe? Did you take time to decide on an order for presenting the details, or did you just list them randomly?
- *Process.* Have you divided the process into enough steps to make it clear, yet not so many that the result is tedious and difficult to read? Have you left out any steps? Are the steps explained clearly and arranged in the proper order so that readers can understand the process?
- *Analysis.* Are there enough elements to thoroughly analyze your idea or object? Does each element in your analysis relate to the whole? Do you need a summary to tie together the elements of your analysis?
- *Classification.* Are your examples classified into categories on the basis of common characteristics? Can each example be placed into one of the categories? Do all the categories of your classification relate to your purpose?
- *Comparison and contrast.* Does your comparison stress important similarities? Does your contrast stress important differences? If you are pointing out both similarities and differences, are the separations clear? If there are many specific comparisons or contrasts, did you give them point by point? If there are few general ones, did you present them in the block method?
- *Analogy.* Is your analogy a true one? Did you limit the analogy to the most important similarities, or did you try to include them all?
- *Definition.* Did you clearly distinguish the subject of your definition from all similar things? What other techniques or patterns did you use to develop your definition? Did you use them effectively?

- *Illustration.* Are your examples specific and interesting? Did you supply enough examples to make your generalization convincing or your abstraction clear? Did you use visual examples to clarify your writing?
- *Cause and effect.* If you are reasoning from effect to cause, have you considered all possible causes? Have you distinguished between immediate causes and necessary conditions? If you are reasoning from a cause to future effects, have you provided sufficient evidence that the effects are likely to result from that cause?
- *Argument.* Have you supplied enough specific information and evidence to support your proposition or conclusion? Do you answer the main arguments against your position? Have you avoided fallacies in your argument?

(It might help to review the discussion of your pattern of development in Step Three.)

Reconsider the order you used to organize your writing. Perhaps you made a poor choice. For example, you may have decided to begin with your most important and interesting material and to use the rest of the material in anticlimactic order. On rereading, you find that the draft loses steam. Try reversing the order of your points, so the most powerful comes last. In fact, unless you really must use chronological or spatial order, climactic is the one to turn to.

Reconsider the pattern of development. Perhaps you set out to compare and contrast two soap operas, and kept at it throughout your draft. On rereading, however, you find that most of what you've written concerns only one of the programs; you dragged in the other from time to time because you were determined to write a comparison. You can probably improve the draft simply by cutting out the references to the program you really don't know enough about and then revising your outline and draft as a straight analysis of the other one.

PARAGRAPHS

During freewriting, you may have divided your draft into paragraphs, or you may not have. Now is the time to paragraph—and to make sure you do it well.

Every paragraph should have a single purpose. Most paragraphs have a main idea that is like an essay's controlling idea, but much narrower. The main idea is usually stated in a *topic sentence*, which is often the first sentence in a paragraph. The topic sentence helps you decide which facts, ideas, and details to include in the paragraph, thus avoiding digressions. When every sentence in a paragraph supports the topic sentence, the paragraph is *unified*. And if there is enough information in the paragraph to make it interesting and the topic sentence convincing, the paragraph is *well developed*. Additionally, when the information in the paragraph is arranged in the best possible pattern and order and the sentences are clearly related to one another, often with transitions, the paragraph is *coherent*.

To identify paragraphs as you read through your draft, look for sentences that say something both important and general about the controlling idea. These are candidates for topic sentences. Then look for a cluster of sentences nearby that provide specific information about the topic sentence. That's probably the rest of the paragraph.

Before each paragraph's first sentence, mark the symbol ¶. Do this even if you've been writing your draft in paragraphs and indenting each one. You'll be surprised how often you change your mind about where paragraph divisions fall.

Some paragraphs don't have main ideas or topic sentences. Some are created just to emphasize a point or to break up a long page of writing. Some are used for transition, to give the reader a resting point between complex ideas.

Paragraphing is in many ways an individual choice. Sometimes, you'll have to paragraph by "feel," which isn't easy. Look for changes of direction in the flow of sentences. In a narrative, for instance, consider starting a new paragraph when a new person enters the story or the action shifts to a different location. In a description, when the observer's view shifts, you can shift to a new paragraph as well.

EXERCISE 5-1

Read the following essay. Then go back and mark the symbol ¶ wherever you believe a paragraph should begin.

The Statue of Liberty, who is almost 100 years old, was conceived as a centennial gift from France, marking our alliance during the Revolution. Edouard de Laboulaye, a French historian, proposed that the monument come from France and the pedestal from the United States. Frédéric Bartholdi, a young Alsatian sculptor, studied the site in New York Harbor and suggested a gigantic statue celebrating the two nations' common heritage of liberty. Using his mother as a model, he began work in Paris in 1874. Enlarging a nine-foot working model four times, he then increased it, section by section, to its height of 151 feet. Alexandre Gustave Eiffel, later to create the famous Paris tower, designed the steel framework with a copper-covered mold. In 1884 the statue was completed and shipped to America in pieces. It cost France $250,000; American efforts to raise a similar amount for the pedestal were stymied by public apathy. Emma Lazarus, who wrote the famous lines now on the statue's base ("Give me your tired, your poor,/Your huddled masses yearning to breathe free") was a tireless fundraiser. So was Joseph Pulitzer, the publisher of the New York *World*. Due in part to their efforts, on October 28, 1886, President Grover Cleveland accepted the "Statue of Liberty Enlightening the World" on behalf of the American people. Over a million visitors a year take the twenty-minute boat ride from Battery Park, at the southern tip of Manhattan, to Liberty Island. The statue looms immense. For the best vantage point, you can ride the elevator ten stories to the top of the pedestal. Here you can study massive details of the 225-ton body and the symbols of liberty: broken shackles at her feet, the tablet in her left hand—inscribed July 4, 1776—and her torch, held high. From the top of the pedestal, a 168-step staircase spirals twelve more stories within the statue's body and head. Through windows in the crown, thirty people can squeeze in a screened view of the harbor panorama, including a three-mile stretch of New Jersey waterfront called Liberty State Park. Today, wind and water have buffeted the statue's once coppery glow to a soft green patina. By day with her steadfast gaze and majestic presence or by night with her torch and tablet lighted, the lady seems a more powerful symbol of liberty than ever.

Once you've marked your draft for paragraph divisions, use the following checklist to evaluate each paragraph.

✓ **Is each paragraph unified?**
If not:
Move irrelevant facts or details to a paragraph where they fit, or drop them. The following paragraph is not unified, because it includes material unrelated to the main idea. Can you find it?

The year 1968 was one of the most violent of the century for America. That year, the Vietnamese War was at its peak, Martin Luther King and Robert Kennedy were assassinated, and there were riots in Chicago at the Democratic Convention. This was one of several times the Democratic Convention was held in Chicago.

Make sure there is only one main idea in a paragraph, and one topic sentence. If a paragraph begins by developing one idea and then veers off to develop another idea, the paragraph is not unified.

Example:

> <u>Recreational facilities are modest at the hotel.</u> There is no pool or tennis court, just an area for volleyball and other lawn games. <u>The rooms in the hotel are quaint and unusual, so people don't mind doing without the usual luxuries.</u> Our room has a claw-footed bathtub, big enough for two, and an old washstand, which adds to the charm. We like to soak in the tub, dress leisurely, then go down to the dining room for the dinner buffet.

You could divide this paragraph into two unified paragraphs, each based on one of the underlined topic sentences. (However, each paragraph would be very short and not well developed, needing more supporting information and detail; but that's a question to consider later.)

EXERCISE 5-2

Are the following paragraphs unified? If not, revise them.

1. Waterskiing is my favorite sport. I first got up on skis when I was seven and my father took me out on Biscayne Bay. He started the boat and I felt a tremendous surge of energy. Waterskiing combines the speed and excitement of powerboating with the soothing quality of the water. I also enjoy water sports such as surfing, water polo, and sailing.

2. I enjoyed my daily routine last summer in Paris. Every morning I'd walk to the bakery on the corner for hot croissants. Then, on my way to school, I'd stop and speak French with the children in the park. The park was one of the most beautiful I have ever seen. In the afternoon, I'd sip coffee in the local cafe and survey the scene. Even though I knew her for only two months, I will never forget my friend Annette.

✔ **Is each paragraph well developed?**
If not:
Add more information, ideas, details, or arguments to support the main idea. You may find what you need in the notes you created in Step Two but

didn't use in your draft. If not, go back to Step Two and brainstorm for more material to flesh out your paragraphs.

Remove any poorly developed paragraphs. When freewriting the draft, you included ideas and statements because you thought they might be useful, or perhaps just so you could keep writing. Now you may find that some of them are dead ends. If they don't contribute much to your controlling idea, and you can't add anything to develop them, cross them out.

You may discover a group of sentences that look like a paragraph but are all general statements—that is, candidates for topic sentences for a series of paragraphs. If you develop each into a paragraph, you could easily double the length of the draft. That would probably make you change your controlling idea and rethink your organization. Instead, you could remove the cluster of generalities and adjust your controlling idea to fit what's left of the draft.

✔ Is each paragraph coherent?

If not:

Make sure each paragraph follows a pattern that fits its purpose and the purpose of the entire piece of writing. In Step Three, you decided on a pattern of development and an order that suited your controlling idea and statement of purpose. Each paragraph should fit into your chosen pattern and order. And each paragraph should have a pattern and order of its own. (Sometimes, like the essay as a whole, there may be a combination of patterns within a paragraph.)

Some patterns that are especially useful for developing paragraphs include:

- *Illustration.* An excellent way to support a topic sentence is with one or more examples.

  Tall teenagers who have grown very quickly are often the least likely to be good basketball players, despite their height. I'll never forget when I went out for the high school basketball team. The coach said that you shoot lay-ups from the right side of the basket with your right hand and from the left side with your left hand. I was almost tall enough to reach the basket without jumping, but I was clumsy. The idea of making lay-ups at all—with either hand— seemed impossible.

- *Analysis.* Another way to support a topic sentence is with analysis— taking a complex object or idea and breaking it down into parts.

  Several factors are needed to ensure the success of a restaurant. For one thing, the atmosphere should be pleasant: elegant or escapist. Also, the service should be efficient—but you shouldn't be too aware of it. There should be value; you should feel the experience is worth the cost. And, of course, the food should be good—perhaps a little more attractive and interesting than you're used to.

- *Comparison and Contrast.* You can also support your topic sentences by presenting similarities and differences.

    The political and moral atmosphere of the early 1980s is similar to that of the early 1950s. Then, there was a conservative in the White House; today, there is another. Then, there was the censoring influence of Senator Joe McCarthy; today, there is the censoring influence of the Moral Majority. The atmosphere on college campuses is also much the same: get ahead.

- *Listing.* One way to support a topic sentence is to supply a series of facts, reasons, or details.

    I like candy for several reasons. It's delicious. It's convenient. It's full of energy. It *isn't* good for you. (Since I don't have many vices, it makes me feel just a bit wicked.)

- *Question and Answer.* One way to involve your readers is to begin a paragraph with a question; the rest of the paragraph supplies the answer. You may offer several answers, with the most important or recent one last, or you may offer one answer, which you develop with reasons or examples.

    Why are soft contact lenses so popular? They are inexpensive and easy to wear. Also, unlike glasses, they conform to the shape of your eyes so there are no vision gaps. Practically, they don't get steamed up when you eat spaghetti or smashed when you play tennis. They don't slip down your nose when you read. And you look more natural.

- *Narration, Description.* Some kinds of paragraphs have no topic sentence, just as some kinds of writing have no controlling idea. A paragraph that narrates or describes gets its coherence by following one of the kinds of order discussed in Step Three: chronological for a narrative paragraph, spatial or climactic for a descriptive paragraph. Here is a narrative paragraph in chronological order:

    It was one-thirty in the morning and no one was around. The streetlight was out so the area was dark. As I walked I heard what I thought at first was the echo of my footsteps, but when I stopped suddenly I still heard the noise. I sensed danger and started running.

EXERCISE 5-3

Identify the pattern of each of the following paragraphs. If a paragraph is not well developed or if any part of a paragraph is out of order, revise the paragraph accordingly.

1. Ireland is a wonderful country to drive through. First, there are picturesque roads with few cars. Second, all signs are in English. Third, since Ireland is a small country, you can cover quite a bit of it in a short time. Fourth, you can enjoy the local villages—and their pubs. And last, you can stay at charming farms or imposing castles. Just plan your itinerary with overnight stops in mind.

2. If antique furniture is well crafted, it will increase in value. I bought a painted oak table years ago for $20. I stripped it to its natural finish and polished it with beeswax. Yesterday, a man offered me fifteen times what I paid for it.

3. The differences between a sun-ripened tomato and one grown in a greenhouse for supermarkets are very obvious. The sun-ripened tomato is red, fragrant, and juicy. Its flavor is rich and tangy, especially if you pick it, still warm, right off the plant.

Use transitional words between sentences (and between paragraphs) to show the connections and relationships between them. You may have the ideas and facts in the right order, but the sentences may not hang together. Try reading your writing aloud. If the paragraphs are choppy and disjointed, add transitions. Transitions include:

- *connective words and expressions*, such as:

after	consequently	moreover	thus
also	even so	nevertheless	till
although	first	next	unless
and	for example	since	when
because	hence	so	while
before	however	then	
but	if	therefore	

Example:

World's Fairs, like the Knoxville Fair in 1982 and the New Orleans Fair in 1984, offer several bonuses for the host city. For example, the free publicity that is sent around the world results in large increases in tourism. <u>Consequently</u>, private enterprise responds to the enlarged demands for food, housing, and other services, and the city's economy prospers. <u>Then, after</u> the fair is over, the buildings and grounds continue to be used for the recreation of the local population.

- *demonstrative pronouns*, which refer to a previous noun:

    that   this   these   those

Example:

Today many students want to attend business school. <u>That</u> is one way to achieve a high-paying career after college.

- *other pronouns that refer to previous nouns:*

another	her	its	she
each	hers	many	some
either	him	neither	their
everyone	his	one	them
he	it	others	they

Example:

The standard pattern of attending college is changing. Most students try to finish college in four years. <u>Many</u> succeed. <u>Others</u>, however, prefer to take a year to work or travel or broaden <u>their</u> experience before completing college. Still other students don't go to college right after high school because <u>they</u> are not motivated or because of <u>their</u> economic circumstances. <u>Many</u> of <u>them</u> enroll in college years later.

Repeat words, phrases, or synonyms throughout the paragraph.

Many <u>record companies</u> are <u>investing</u> in varied <u>entertainment areas</u>, such as <u>cable television</u> and <u>videotape cassettes</u>. <u>RCA</u> has invested in <u>videocassettes</u>, <u>videodisks</u>, and <u>cable television</u>. <u>Columbia</u> is another <u>record company</u> that has involved itself in new <u>areas</u> by expanding into the growing leisure and electronics <u>entertainment</u> market.

Use transitional paragraphs. In writing that is long or complex, transitional paragraphs give readers a chance to pause, think about what they've just read, and tie it to what is coming. Typically, transitional paragraphs summarize what has been written and suggest what follows. They are often composed of one or two sentences.

So Ford had revolutionized the automotive industry with his assembly-line approach. What effect did this have on other industries?

EXERCISE 5-4

Underline the transitions in the following two paragraphs. Show where additional transitions would be helpful, and if possible, provide them.

1.   Hang-gliding has been around for a long while. John Montgomery balloon-launched a hang-glider near San Diego ninety years ago. England's Percy Pilcher glided for over two minutes a few years later in a crow-tailed glider. Otto Lebenthal used a cambered-wing biplane. Octave Chanute developed a double-decker design, borrowed and refined for power flight by the Wright brothers. Francis Rogallo, in 1948, patented the first limp-wing form using a kite towed behind a boat. Richard Miller, in 1964, built the first free hang-glider.

2.   In San Jose, California, there is a weird mansion. Each of its rooms is unusual. For example, one has skylights in the floor, one has four fireplaces, and one has upside-down furniture. The stairways are strange also. Some end in ceilings, while others end in walls. One stairway leads down to a landing from which you cannot exit. When you reach the bottom, you have to turn around and go back up.

Avoid overlong paragraphs. Most paragraphs need a topic sentence supported by specific details. Be careful, though, not to carry paragraph development too far by cramming everything even remotely connected to the topic sentence into one paragraph. If a paragraph is too long, readers tend to lose concentration because they have no chance to pause and absorb the ideas. Very long paragraphs look intimidating and discourage reading.

If you write a paragraph of half a typed page or more, chances are that you can divide it. An obvious place is just before a transitional word, especially a word such as *but* or *however* that signals a change of angle. The transitional word will then connect the flow of thoughts from paragraph to paragraph.

Sometimes you may want to divide a paragraph just to emphasize a point. Putting an idea or fact into its own paragraph gives it more attention. Even a one-sentence paragraph is acceptable, if it is preceded or followed by paragraphs that clarify it.

. . . Their confrontations have been classic battles of two opposites that bring out the best in each.

And the fact remains: Björn Borg and John McEnroe have an almost balanced record of wins and losses in their matches.

This might be explained by several factors. . . .

OPENING, ENDING, TITLE

Like other paragraphs in a draft, the opening and ending must be carefully revised. Often, it is a good idea to wait until you've finished improving content, organization, and paragraph structure so that you can strengthen the opening and ending in the light of revisions you made in other parts of your draft.

A title can occur to you at any point in the writing process. Sometimes, you may think of one as you are prewriting; at other times, you may need to wait until you have a clearer sense of where your writing is headed. If you have not yet provided a title, revision is a good time to think about one because you are now considering your draft as a whole.

✔ Does the draft have an effective opening?

Some writing—personal letters, business memos—requires no special opening. The reader just plunges in. But in most other writing, at least a sentence is needed to get readers interested. Often at least a paragraph is needed to "hook" their attention. The opening paragraph should be written with special care. If it's wordy or boring, the reader may not go on.

If the draft does not have an effective opening:
Write a new introduction or revise the existing one. Here are some suggestions:

- *Tell the reader what's coming.* Readers want to know what you're writing about. In most practical writing, state the topic in the first paragraph, as well as the controlling idea if you have one. Sometimes you may hold the controlling idea until later or, if it is so controversial or technical that it may stop your readers cold, until the end. But otherwise, lead off with it.

  Has the United Nations become a forum for politics rather than diplomacy? A study of resolutions passed during the last five years will show that it has.

- *Show the relevance of your topic.* Readers want to know why they should read what you've written: "What's in it for me?" Consider what you know about your readers. Are you writing about something very new or very specialized? Your readers may know little about it and care less. Your introduction can show them why they should care, and how the topic relates to their lives.

A high unemployment rate means that many people who want to work are without jobs—and without income. Unemployment can be devastating to someone trying to pay a mortgage or feed a family. People who are employed are also affected because the whole economy suffers: spending lessens, production drops, tax revenues decrease. Thus, it's important to understand the factors leading to high unemployment and to learn what we can do to avoid them.

- *Start with a significant or surprising statement or question,* as in this introduction to an analysis of New York's problems with the federal government.

Did you know that more people live in New York City than in the twelve smallest states in the Union put together? But those states send twenty-four senators to Washington, while New York City sends none.

- *Give an example or tell a story that is interesting in itself and leads into your topic or controlling idea.*

One summer I traveled third class on a Turkish maritime ship between Haifa and Istanbul. My cabin was about as big as a closet. Whenever we anchored, the cabin shook as the anchor chain rattled loudly on the other side of the thin wall. But, despite the cramped conditions and simple food, it was the best trip I ever took. Traveling on a budget can be fun—and it is certainly better than staying home.

EXERCISE 5-5

Using the suggestions given in the preceding section, improve the following openings.

1. Let us sample the following comments to get an idea of the problem being caused by cutbacks in student aid and what, perhaps, can be done about it.
2. Polls may sometimes be inaccurate by several percentage points; however, 53 percent of the people in a recent poll believed that the president would be reelected, while 42 percent believed he would not and 5 percent were undecided.
3. The price of gold fluctuates a great deal depending on many factors. Some of these factors have been at work during the past few years to raise and lower the price of gold to record levels. In this paper, we will

look at some of the factors that have contributed to the fluctuations
and what caused these fluctuations.

✔ Does the draft have an effective ending?

Sometimes a piece of writing stops naturally. But if it stops abruptly or
leaves readers dangling, add an ending. And if an ending is wordy or dull,
improve it. Remember, the ending of a piece of writing often leaves a lasting
impression on readers because it is the last part that they see.

If the draft does not have an effective ending:
Write a new ending, or revise the existing one. Here are some suggestions:

- *Summarize.* If your writing is long and complex, a brief summary of
  the main facts or arguments can help your readers understand it as a
  whole.

  There are several ways, then, to cut down on refined sugar: by substituting
  honey or artificial sweeteners; by cutting your intake in half; by reading labels
  and avoiding presweetened foods; and by substituting fruits and vegetables for
  sugary desserts and snacks.

- *Restate the controlling idea.* By the time your readers reach the end of
  your writing, they may welcome a reminder of what you set out to explain or prove. Wrap it up, if you can, with a fresh—and memorable—
  restatement of your point.

  So the daughter of the star who never found that happy place "somewhere
  over the rainbow" is a star who has found it herself.

- *Give a solution or draw a conclusion.* If you've been describing a problem, it's natural to end with a possible solution. If you've been building
  an argument, it's natural to end with a conclusion.

  Because of these problems, which seem unlikely to be resolved, the only solution is to withdraw from the conference.

- *Supply a final, clinching sentence.* If your writing is short or fairly easy
  to understand, a few well-chosen words can bring it to a close. Sometimes you can even use the words of somebody else.

  At some point, all of us have to accept responsibility for our lives and
  actions. As Harry Truman put it, "The buck stops here."

EXERCISE 5-6

Read three articles in magazines or anthologies. Look at the openings and endings. Explain how each works, and state whether you think it is effective.

✓ **Does the draft have a good title?**

Some kinds of writing—college papers, reports, essays—need titles. The title is your first chance to get your readers interested and to start them reading in the right spirit. A good title suggests what's coming and excites interest; it should, of course, be compatible in style and tone with the rest of the paper.

If the draft does not have a title:

Invent a title. Two main types of titles are common in practical writing:

- The *statement* tells in a matter-of-fact way what the writing is about.

  > Animal Imagery in *King Lear*
  > How Beer Is Brewed
  > The Life Cycle of the Frog
  > Exercise Can Be Dangerous to Your Health

  Some papers have titles in two parts, one stating the topic and the other suggesting the controlling idea. Such titles are often used in academic writing, reports, essays, nonfiction books, and newspaper editorials.

  > Theodore Roosevelt after 1908: A Leader without Followers
  > The Nuclear Arms Race: Pathway to Destruction

- The *hook* tries to grab readers who might otherwise not read on. A hook is frequently used in popular writing, especially magazines and tabloid newspapers, and in many nonfiction books, but not usually in academic or formal writing. It can be a phrase, a statement, or a question.

  > Illness for Fun and Profit
  > Where Are You When We Need You, Walter Cronkite?

EXERCISE 5-7

Examine magazines, journals, and anthologies, and find several examples of each of the two kinds of titles—the statement and the hook. Analyze the purpose and controlling idea of each piece of writing. Who is its intended audience? Is each title effective? Why?

SUMMARY

In Step Five—revise—you should:

- Reread your draft carefully and objectively, looking for problems in organization, content, and paragraphing.
- Mark problem areas with a colored pencil and make notes to yourself on the draft that identify problems and suggest solutions.
- Ask yourself the following questions:

> ✔ Does the draft include all the ideas in your outline?
> ✔ Does the draft include all the important material you gathered during prewriting?
> ✔ Does every fact, idea, and argument in the draft relate to your statement of purpose and controlling idea?
> ✔ Have you supplied enough facts and details to support each point?
> ✔ Are your facts, figures, and quotations accurate?
> ✔ Does the draft follow the order of your outline?
> ✔ Are your chosen patterns of development and order effective?
> ✔ Is each paragraph unified, well developed, and coherent?
> ✔ Does the draft have an effective opening and ending and a good title?

- Add, remove, and rearrange material according to your answers to these questions and your penciled notes on the draft.

Remember, even the greatest writers revise their work again and again before they're finally satisfied with it. If you have time, don't go on to Step Six just yet. Take your revised draft and go through Step Five one more time. You will probably discover further improvements that you can make in content and organization.

I have rewritten—often several times—
every word I have ever published. My
pencils outlast their erasures.

VLADIMIR NABOKOV

Step 6: Refine

Think of writing as gold. Now think of poor word choices and mistakes in grammar and spelling as impurities that make the gold worth less. Refining the impurities out of your writing, whether it be a term paper or a job application, makes it more valuable.

Once you are satisfied with the content and organization of your draft, it's time for Step Six—refine. You must go through your writing, word by word and punctuation mark by punctuation mark, to make sure every little detail is correct. Refining makes a big difference, not only in clarity, but in your reader's attitude toward your writing.

Settle down with your draft in the place you work best. You'll need those two writer's tools mentioned in Step Four: a dictionary and a handbook of grammar and usage. The dictionary is an authority on what words mean and how they are spelled. The handbook is an authority on correct sentence structure, capitalization, punctuation, and word usage.

As you refine, remember the advice at the beginning of Step Five: be objective, read carefully, and mark the draft whenever you find something that needs fixing.

MARK YOUR DRAFT

Many writers use standard proofreaders' symbols to mark changes in their drafts. These symbols save time and make the draft easy to read. Here are some examples:

Symbol	Meaning
investigtion ^a	Insert letter.
many think ^people	Insert word.
houston	Capitalize.
Government/Inspector	Use lowercase letters.
presentation	Transpose letters.
to/earnestly/desire/	Transpose words.
he was#here already	Insert space.
he will go to day	Close up.
judgement	Delete a letter and close up.
occasional reports from the members of the committee	Delete words.
stet	Restore the first version (when written next to a word or passage that has been crossed out or changed).

Of course, you may have created your own symbols; if so, use them.

USE A CHECKLIST

Here's a list of questions to ask yourself as you reread and refine the draft. The first group of questions is about style—the general effect of your writing. The second group concerns choosing the right words and keeping your style consistent. The third is about making sentences more effective. The fourth is about mechanics—grammar, punctuation, capitalization, and spelling.

A Checklist for Refining

Style
- ✓ Is the style right for your topic, purpose, and readers?
- ✓ Is the tone right for your topic, purpose, and readers?
- ✓ Are the style and tone consistent?

Words
- ✓ Is each word used precisely?
- ✓ Is each word specific?
- ✓ Are the words appropriate?
- ✓ Are the words fresh?

Sentences
- ✓ Is each sentence clear?
- ✓ Is each sentence concise?
- ✓ Is each sentence vigorous?
- ✓ Are the sentences varied in length and structure?

Mechanics
- ✓ Are the sentences grammatically correct?
- ✓ Are the punctuation and capitalization correct?
- ✓ Are all the words spelled correctly?

STYLE

Many people believe that style can be applied to writing like a coat of paint. But style is individual. It is the way you express yourself in what you say and write. Your own style emerges naturally from the words you choose and the ways you use them. Nobody else speaks or writes just the way you do.

In fact, you probably have several styles. Listen to yourself joking with a child, chatting with a classmate, talking with older people, addressing the judge in traffic court. You use different words in each situation, and you use them in different kinds of sentences. Generally, your style is simple for children, more complicated for adults. It's informal for your classmates and as formal as you can make it for the judge. You make choices when you talk, and you should make them when you write.

In any kind of writing, whoever your reader and whatever your topic and purpose, avoid the following:

- *Wordiness.* Even if you are writing in a formal style, remove unnecessary words. Wordiness bores readers.
- *Obscurity.* Don't use words that are highly technical or overly abstract without explaining them. Your readers must always be able to understand exactly what you mean.
- *Pretentiousness.* Don't show off. The nineteenth-century style of writing may have been effective for a nineteenth-century audience, but it doesn't belong in a term paper or a business letter. Use long or difficult words and elaborate sentences only when you have to, never for decoration.

You can learn something about style by reading other writers, just as you can learn about tennis by watching Chris Evert Lloyd. But it's usually a bad idea to copy another writer's style. Imitative writing won't be as good as the original, and the other writer's style might fit you like somebody else's clothes. Let your reading influence your style; but when you write, be yourself.

✔ **Is the style right for your topic, purpose, and readers?**
If not:
Rewrite in an appropriate style. Long words and sentences create a complex formal style.

> Bear in mind always the magnitude of the need, never evading the responsibility. One must never withdraw one's aid from a worthy cause, nor hesitate even momentarily from proffering it. Now is the time to make your donation.

Slang words and contractions create an informal style; short words and sentences create a simple style.

> Don't forget how much we need. Don't cop out. Don't hang back. You shouldn't pull out of a good thing. Give now.

A middle style, somewhere between formal and informal, mixes long and short sentences and uses words that are neither slangy nor especially long:

> Always remember how great the need is, and live up to your responsibility. Don't delay. You should never stop helping a good cause. Give now.

If your draft is written in an informal style, and you decide to put it in a middle style, you'll need to change some words and reshape some sentences.

(Advice on choosing words and shaping sentences can be found on pages 107–135.)

✔ Is the tone right for your topic, purpose, and readers?

When you talk, you can sound cheerful or angry, friendly or unfriendly, humorous or serious, sincere or sarcastic, objective or emotional. Tone of voice shows your attitude toward your subject and your listener. Tone in writing does the same thing, and it works through your choice of words.

If the tone is not right for your topic, purpose, and readers:
Rewrite in an appropriate tone. When your purpose is to explain, and you don't know your reader personally, you should probably use an impersonal tone. For example:

> Several of the guests who will be honored at the banquet on May 7, including Anita Gonzalez, will not be able to attend. Would it be possible to change the date?

If you are writing to someone you know well, however, an impersonal tone would seem very strange, even unfriendly. Your tone should be more personal:

> I hope you'll consider changing the date of the banquet. Some of the people we'll be honoring (including Anita) won't be able to come on the seventh.

What makes the second version sound friendlier and more personal than the first? It uses more personal pronouns: *I, you, we.* It uses contractions. And the writer does not repeat information the reader knows—Anita's last name and the month of the banquet.

If you want to convince your readers of a point you care deeply about, let your feelings show through in your tone. But don't expect your sincerity to persuade by itself. You must also give your readers a strong argument to think about.

Remember that tone also shows your attitude toward your subject. The next three sentences all say essentially the same thing, but each expresses a different attitude.

OBJECTIVE:	The police officer walked down the street and knocked loudly on the door.
APPROVING:	The police officer strode down the street and rapped firmly on the door.
DISAPPROVING:	The police officer swaggered down the street and pounded rudely on the door.

The sentence that is objectively written simply states what happened. The approving sentence also tells what happened, but it uses words that indicate an attitude—the writer thinks the police officer is bold and decisive. The disapproving sentence tells another story—the writer thinks the police officer is a bully.

As you can see, choosing words carefully is the key to controlling your tone. (Advice on choosing words appears on pages 107–115.)

EXERCISE 6-1

Rewrite sentences 1 and 2 to change the tone from personal to impersonal, or vice versa. Rewrite sentences 3 and 4 to change the objective tone first to approving and then to disapproving.

1. Please inform Dr. Michael Laurence that his application for the position of medical consultant has been approved and that he may assume his new responsibilities at his earliest possible convenience.
2. If upstairs can deliver the funds by the 20th, we'll ditch the manuals and opt for the electrics.
3. The blonde woman smiled, then sat in the chair.
4. The hunter intended to shoot deer.

Rewrite to avoid a sexist tone.   Sexist writing is writing that discriminates against, or unnecessarily excludes, one of the sexes. If you write with a sexist tone, your readers are likely to interpret your attitude as unfriendly and to question the objectivity of your writing. For example:

> Every doctor on call must leave a list of telephone numbers where he can be reached. (Are there no women doctors?)
> Nurses are to wear white stockings on duty. (Including male nurses?)
> One man, one vote. (Don't women vote?)

To avoid a sexist tone:

- Don't assume that certain jobs are always done by men and others by women. Avoid sexual stereotyping.

  All doctors on call must leave a list of telephone numbers where they can be reached.
  Female nurses are to wear white stockings on duty, and male nurses are to wear white socks.

- Don't use *man* when referring to all humanity. Use *men and women,* or *people,* or *human beings,* or *everybody.*
- Don't use *girl* when you mean *woman.*
- Be consistent in referring to males and females. Use first names and initials or titles consistently.

  I have to talk to Jon Miller, Carl Smith, and Patricia Jones.
  I have to talk to Mr. Miller, Mr. Smith, and Ms. Jones.
  I have to talk to Miller, Smith, and Jones.

- Unless you know the sex of the recipient, avoid using "Dear Sir" or "Dear Madam" in writing a business letter. Whenever possible, use the person's title instead—for example, "Dear Credit Manager."
- Avoid using masculine pronouns when referring to both men and women.

  Each student should bring his registration form to Old Main next Monday.

This suggests that all of the students are male. If they're not, here are some ways to solve the problem:

—Use a plural subject.

  All students should bring their registration forms to Old Main next Monday.

—Use both masculine and feminine pronouns.

  Each student should bring his or her registration form to Old Main next Monday.

—Use the second-person pronouns, *you* and *your.*

  To all students: Bring your registration form to Old Main next Monday.

—Avoid pronouns.

  Each student should bring the registration form to Old Main next Monday.

EXERCISE 6-2

Rewrite the following sentences to avoid a sexist tone.

1. Any employee who will not reach his sixty-fifth birthday by May 1 is eligible.
2. The girl at the reception desk will give you the folders.

3. Each participant must furnish his own birth certificate.
4. Each participant in the chili competition should submit her recipe to the judges.
5. Mankind will benefit from the company's invention.
6. Mr. Roth, Mr. Beck, and Fran Weiler are in charge of preparations.

✔ **Are the style and tone consistent?**

If not:

Eliminate abrupt shifts in style and tone. If your style is formal, keep it that way throughout the draft; don't drop in a few slang words here and there. If your tone is serious through most of the draft, don't start cracking jokes in the next-to-last-paragraph. Your readers will wonder not only what you're up to but also whether you know what you're doing.

To test whether your style and tone are consistent, read the draft aloud in the tone of voice that fits it, and listen for any words or sentences that sound out of place. Here's an example:

> Many animals are on the endangered species list. By the end of this century, many species of birds, mammals, and reptiles that share our earth today will be gone forever. To avoid these total wipeouts, we must be careful how we use the environment.

The passage is written in a middle style, but the expression "total wipeouts" is slang. The word *extinctions* would provide both the right meaning and the right level of formality for the passage.

EXERCISE 6-3

Rewrite the following paragraph as necessary to eliminate any inconsistencies in style or tone.

> Scuba diving is my newest hobby. I began by snorkeling but soon found that staring down from above just isn't where it's at. Descending to the depth of the angelfish and brushing up against the coral is positively mind blowing. And the lower I dive, the higher I feel. In fact, one might describe scuba diving as a rapturous experience of fathomless dimension.

WORDS

While writing your draft, you didn't allow yourself to be slowed down by worries about word choice. Now that you've reread the draft and thought about its style and tone, some words may seem inappropriate, or, at least, better words can be found. This is the time to find better words—and to fill in any blanks.

✔ **Is each word used precisely?**
If not:
Check the word's literal meaning, or denotation, in a dictionary. Many words have similar meanings. For instance, *murder, manslaughter, assassination,* and *execution* all indicate the killing of a person, but they're not interchangeable. If you're not certain that you've used a word precisely, look the word up in your dictionary. If the definition doesn't agree with what you want to say, then look at the synonyms given for the word. In most dictionaries, you'll find some other words with similar meanings and a discussion that will help you choose the right one for your purpose.

Sometimes you may write down a word that sounds or looks like the word you want:

> Sandra Day O'Connor is an *imminent* Supreme Court justice.
> The accident *effected* Jean so much that she had nightmares for a year.

The word *imminent* sounds right, but it means "about to happen." The writer wanted to say *eminent*, which means "distinguished." And *effected*, meaning "caused to happen," should be replaced by *affected*, which means "emotionally moved."

EXERCISE 6-4

Look up the meanings of the italicized words that follow. Are they used correctly? If not, find a more precise word.

1. The doctor seemed *disinterested* in her patient's latest complaints.
2. My old grandmother used to tell us *incredulous* ghost stories.
3. A train is a *nostalgic* means of travel.

4. Wimbledon is a *reverential* tennis tournament.
5. Equal pay for equal work is a goal of the *feminine* movement.
6. After the team lost three games in a row, the players' *morality* was sinking.

Be sensitive to the word's emotional associations, or connotations. The words *residence* and *home* denote about the same thing, but *residence* is formal and unemotional, while *home* is loaded with emotion. The connotations of the words you choose are part of your tone.

Words that are emotionally right for one purpose may be quite wrong for another. For instance, your best friend can teasingly say that you are *scatterbrained,* but if someone else used that word you might resent it. *Disorganized,* maybe, or *unsystematic,* but not *scatterbrained.*

Different people often interpret the same word differently. To someone living in San Diego or Miami, *January* may suggest mild, pleasant weather. To New Englanders, it may suggest cold and ice. So be aware of who your readers are, and consider how they will react to your word choice.

EXERCISE 6-5

Analyze the connotations of the italicized words in the following sentences. Which ones don't fit the context well? Replace them with words that do.

1. You look so *skinny;* it's obvious your diet has been a success.
2. When making policy changes, a president should be *stubborn* rather than indecisive.
3. My friend is so *filthy* that he drops his clothes in piles around the room.
4. The lemon meringue pie was pleasantly *sour.*
5. The supervisor is so *thrifty* that he takes paper towels home from the company washroom.

✔ **Is each word specific?**

If you write, "We talked about an important issue," that's too general and vague to be either interesting or informative. You might have been discussing the Middle East, the weather forecast, or who should pay for the hamburgers.

If the words you use are not specific:
Use specific nouns and verbs. If you were eating cherries, write *cherries*, not *fruit*. If you were conversing loudly, write *shout* rather than *talk*. Give your reader the clearest possible picture: for example, "As they waited for the debate to begin, the candidates bickered about who would speak first."

Using specific nouns and verbs lets you avoid long strings of other words, such as adjectives and adverbs, for clarification. Move from the general to the specific:

```
General ──────────────────────────────────────────────→ Specific
animal ──────────────→ dog ──────────────→ hound ──────────────→ beagle
go ──────────────────────→ run ──────────────────→ sprint
```

Of course, there are times when you must make general statements. For instance, your controlling idea is usually a generalization. The topic sentence of a paragraph may also be very general. But you must eventually get down to specifics, or you'll confuse and bore your readers.

EXERCISE 6-6

Number the nouns in each of the following columns from most general (*1*) to most specific (*4*).

basketball player	vehicle	building	course
L. A. Laker	MGB	hotel	meal
Magic Johnson	automobile	Waldorf-Astoria	dessert
athlete	sports car	residence	dinner

Use concrete rather than abstract words. A concrete word refers to what you can see, hear, touch, smell, or taste. An abstract word refers to a concept that the mind can understand but the senses can't perceive. Here are some examples:

Abstract	*Concrete*
having fun	throwing a Frisbee
beautiful	Crater Lake
evil	the Holocaust
sharp	razor
It tasted terrible.	It tasted like old athletic socks.
I felt sad.	I cried.

Sometimes you have to use abstract terms. There are no concrete words for the idea that "Canada is a democracy." But you can use concrete details to help your readers understand the abstraction. What kind of government does Canada have? Who are the public officials, and how are they elected? These are questions with concrete answers.

As you read your draft, underline the abstract words. For example:

> Apricot was a <u>crazy</u> dog.

Then try to substitute concrete words or add concrete details to make your point. Try to appeal to your reader's senses of sight, sound, taste, touch, and smell.

> Apricot, a strange mixture of dachshund and miniature collie, would charge at anyone who came through the front door, snapping with his sharp white teeth at any ankle or hand that moved.

The first sentence only gives the writer's opinion of Apricot. The second sentence shows Apricot in action and lets readers form their own opinion.

EXERCISE 6-7

Add concrete details to make the following sentences more vivid.

1. I built a fire in the fireplace.
2. Rand drank a glass of fruit juice.
3. My brother is lazy.
4. Stuart cut some flowers.
5. The house needed repairs.
6. Carol and Steve washed their hair in a waterfall.

Cut back on vague qualifiers. General words and phrases such as *very*, *a little*, *most*, and *few* are often used to narrow down the meaning of another word. Often, however, a more specific word or expression does the job better and more economically.

Vague	Specific
a lot of money	five million dollars
a little while ago	a week ago
most drivers	three out of four drivers
a few children	a boy and two girls
He was very happy.	He was elated.

Sometimes, a vague qualifier appears in a sentence although the meaning of the sentence requires no qualifier at all. In such cases, omit the qualifier.

I am *very* certain the ambassador will resign.
I am certain the ambassador will resign.

EXERCISE 6-8

In the following sentences, either replace the vague qualifiers with more specific words, omit them, or, if possible, rewrite the sentence using concrete verbs and nouns.

1. *Most* club members favor raising dues *a little*.
2. Josh is *quite* thin and *somewhat* nervous.
3. That executive made *a lot* of money in *many* enterprises.
4. Barbra Streisand is *very* right for the part.
5. Can we meet at *around* dinnertime?
6. The tenants ran *extremely* quickly from the burning building.

✔ **Are the words appropriate?**
When choosing words, consider your topic, purpose, and reader.
If the words are inappropriate:
Replace words that are too informal. You might use slang when talking with a friend. However, you don't usually see it in writing or hear it during network newscasts. For example:

Hey, he's a loser.
Can you dig it?

Slang like this may be just as clear and precise—for people who use it—as any other words in the language. But two things are wrong with it: some people don't understand it, and some people who do understand it may be offended by its informality and without thinking reject an otherwise serious piece of writing.

Avoid words that are pompous. Many people believe that long or unusual words make their prose more impressive. However, they usually sound stilted and pretentious. For example, crooks are called "perpetrators." Bureaucrats would rather "utilize" something than use it. A lawyer would rather "ascertain what eventuated" than find out what happened. When a television station's equipment breaks down, it is "experiencing momentary technical difficulties." As an airplane comes in for landing, the flight attendant asks passengers to "extinguish all smoking materials."

In any writing you do, choose the words that best say what you mean. For a given topic, purpose, and reader, a long and difficult word may in fact be the most appropriate choice. But if two words—one more familiar than the other—are exact synonyms, the more common word is usually the one to use. With a common word, you know for sure that your meaning will be understood.

Here are some more choices:

Pompous	*Simple*
cognizant	aware
endeavor	try
facilitate	help
implement	begin, carry out
initiate	begin
prior to	before
subsequent to	after
terminate	end
transmit	send

EXERCISE 6-9

Here are some phrases that would be inappropriate in most practical writing. Identify the problem in each, and change the phrase to one that more clearly conveys the same meaning.

ameliorate the situation	expiration of the period
as you deem appropriate	foxy
attempt to procure	hereby and hereinafter
bad vibes	mucho macho
cop out	pig out
dude	pursuant to the letter
endeavor to ascertain	rendering every possible assistance

Can you add any others?

Avoid jargon. Technical or specialized vocabulary is necessary for many professionals to do their jobs. A doctor writing for an audience of professional colleagues wouldn't say simply that a patient had a heart attack. The audience would expect—and be able to understand—a more detailed diagnosis, such as the patient experienced an "infarction of the left ventricle."

But this kind of vocabulary, called *jargon*, can baffle people who don't understand it. So, when writing for general readers, a doctor would probably use the expression *heart attack* and describe it in ordinary words.

Writers sometimes use jargon merely to impress readers with their knowledge. They borrow legal and business terms, computerese, psychological and scientific terms, and sports slang to dress up language that they think sounds too ordinary. A committee becomes a "task force," a meeting an "interface," and fear "paranoia." Unfortunately, such usage usually results in loss of clarity.

Following are some examples of jargon that are often used in general writing when a simpler term would be much clearer.

burned-out	gridlock	orient, orientate (verbs)
conceptual framework	hard data	parameter
coping strategy	holistic	productivity
crisis-oriented	impact (verb)	program (verb)
decision model	implement (verb)	role-playing
dynamics	input	scenario
feedback	leading edge	shortfall
game plan	learning experience	state of the art
glitch	orchestrate	syndrome

EXERCISE 6-10

Define these jargon terms, and identify the fields they come from. For each, provide a simpler term that a general audience would understand.

countdown	load the bases
game plan	manic-depressive
interpose no objection	repressed hostility
latent alienation	run with the ball

Avoid coinages. A new word doesn't appear like magic. Somewhere, somebody coined it—made it up by combining words ("Reaganomics," "Pac-Maniac") or by adding a prefix ("*hyper*hits," "*vid*kids") or a suffix ("plant*nap-ping*," "legal*ese*"). Newsmagazines coin such expressions constantly. Most coinages, however, are short-lived. Here's a sentence using a recent coinage.

> The town board has approved the plan to *condominiumize* the abandoned warehouse.

Rewritten in clear English:

> The town board has approved the plan to convert the abandoned warehouse into condominiums.

Don't guess at words. When you can't quite remember a word, guessing at it can result in sentences like this:

> They arrived late because of their *unableness* to get the car started.

The correct word, of course, is *inability*; there's no such word as *unableness*.

If you can, look up words you're not sure of in a dictionary. Otherwise, write the sentence another way.

> They arrived late because the car wouldn't start.

EXERCISE 6-11

Rewrite these sentences, replacing the coinages and "guessed-at" words with ordinary English.

1. Unless we prioritize our activities, we'll have a minidisaster on our hands.
2. The inprecedented increase in crime is a sad-but-truism.
3. Many professional athletes earn megabucks.
4. Children of alumni are given preferentiality over other applicants.
5. Dollar-wise, you're better off shopping at a discounterium.

Use abbreviations sensibly. If you are writing about the North Atlantic Treaty Organization it's a waste of your time and a burden on your reader's patience to spell the name out every time. After you have mentioned it once, you can use the standard abbreviation NATO consistently. However, you should always spell out a name before using its abbreviation unless you can be absolutely sure that every reader will understand what the abbreviation refers to.

Avoid clichés. Clichés are phrases that may once have been striking and fresh but have lost their effectiveness through overuse. Clichés may save us the trouble of creating new expressions, but they also make writing sound tired and dull. Some clichés are figures of speech ("clear as crystal"); others are standardized expressions ("last but not least"). What all clichés have in common, however, is that they bore readers and thus weaken writing.

Here are some clichés. Can you think of others?

acid test	eyeball to eyeball	new avenues are being
along these lines	few and far between	explored
as a matter of course	first and foremost	new dimension
at the crossroads	goes without saying	on tne back burner
at this point in time	growing body of	render inoperable
be that as it may	evidence	replete with interest
belabor the point	gut feeling	sadder but wiser
bite the bullet	hard data	scratch the surface
bottom line	in-depth study	spin-off value
burning question	in the final analysis	the art and science
by leaps and bounds	in this day and age	threshold of a new
by the same token	it's safe to say	idea
conspicuous by its	leaves much to be	tip of the iceberg
absence	desired	undertake a study
contrary to popular	let's check the record	uphill climb
opinion	looms large	venture the opinion
crash program	measure of success	view with alarm
cutting edge	mount an attack	warrants further
decision-making	multifaceted problem	investigation
doomed to failure	neither rhyme nor	ways and means
easier said than done	reason	words fail to express

SENTENCES

Good sentences share a few basic qualities. First, they should be *clear.* Your readers must understand what you mean. If you have already refined your choice of words, the problem in an unclear sentence lies somewhere else—perhaps in the sentence structure.

Sentences should be *concise,* with no needless words or phrases. They should be *vigorous,* with verbs that show action. And they should be *varied in their length and structure*—sometimes long and complex, sometimes short and simple.

✓ **Is each sentence clear?**

If not:

Keep related parts of a sentence together. If they are separated, their relationship and the meaning of the sentence become unclear. For example, when a modifier is separated from the word that it modifies, the sentence can be confusing—and sometimes even ridiculous.

> UNCLEAR: I ordered a camera from the catalog with a built-in flash.
>
> CLEAR: I ordered a camera with a built-in flash from the catalog.

Sometimes the position of a modifier makes it impossible for the reader to tell which part of the sentence is being modified.

> Running frequently can result in weight loss.

To clear up the ambiguity, reposition the modifier so that it clearly belongs with one part of the sentence, or recast the sentence.

> Frequently, running can result in weight loss.
> Running can frequently result in weight loss.
>   *or*
> Frequent running can result in weight loss.

EXERCISE 6-12

Clarify the following sentences by putting the related parts together.

1. Nicole makes pizza for her boyfriend with anchovies on top.
2. The studio apartment only was shown this morning.
3. Jean lifted a weight in the gym that was over a hundred pounds.
4. Local radio stations now play country music throughout America.
5. Ed ate caviar on his birthday, which cost fifty dollars.
6. The president said after the meeting he would make a formal announcement.

Be sure that pronoun reference is clear. Make sure a pronoun refers clearly to its antecedent, the noun it's standing in for. If there is any doubt, repeat the original noun or rewrite the sentence to avoid the confusion.

> FIRST VERSION: Clive called Bernard once a week when he was studying in London. (Was Clive or Bernard studying in London?)
>
> REVISIONS: Clive called Bernard once a week when Clive was studying in London.

When Clive was studying in London, he called Bernard once a week.

When Bernard was studying in London, Clive called him once a week.

EXERCISE 6-13

Revise the following sentences to make the pronoun reference clear.

1. As the robbers put their guns down, the police grabbed them.
2. Rachel told Jessica that she had to leave.
3. Make a copy of that letter, and put it in the file.
4. Uncle Art agreed with Uncle Ned that his tie was atrocious.
5. Dentists and doctors receive similar training, but the public views them with less respect.

Don't leave out necessary words or phrases. Because you write a draft steadily, without stopping to correct, you may leave out parts of a sentence that are necessary for clarity. Now you must add those parts.

UNCLEAR: Jane dislikes him more than Arthur.
CLEAR: Jane dislikes him more than she *dislikes* Arthur.
      or
Jane dislikes him more than Arthur *does.*

UNCLEAR: Plays here are as expensive as Broadway.
CLEAR: Plays here are as expensive as *they are on* Broadway.

UNCLEAR: Chicago has and always will be my home.
CLEAR: Chicago has *been* and always will be my home.

EXERCISE 6-14

Supply the omitted words to make the following sentences clearer.

1. The Pacific is larger than any ocean.
2. Rowayne has always and always will be a perfectionist.
3. Mr. Robbins paid me more than Adam.
4. The elephants eat more peanuts than monkeys.
5. My mother treated me more kindly than my father.
6. Some hotels in Atlantic City are bigger than Las Vegas.

Eliminate unnecessary shifts in person, number, and tense. Unless grammar or meaning requires a shift, a sentence should be consistent in person (first person, second person, or third person), number (singular or plural), and tense (present, past, or future). Unnecessary shifts in any of these elements can confuse meaning and make reading difficult.

SHIFT: If *students* want to work in the lab on weekends, *you* must obtain *your* instructor's permission. (shift from third person to second person)

BETTER: If *students* want to work in the lab on weekends, *they* must obtain *their* instructor's permission.

     or

     If *you* want to work in the lab on weekends, *you* must obtain *your* instructor's permission.

SHIFT: I prefer driving a small *car* because *they* are easy to park on city streets. (shift from singular to plural)

BETTER: I prefer driving a small *car* because *it* is easy to park on city streets.

     or

     I prefer driving small *cars* because *they* are easy to park on city streets.

SHIFT: Although thirty seconds *remained* on the clock, the fans *pour* out of the stands and *tear* down the goalposts. (shift from past tense to present tense)

BETTER: Although thirty seconds *remained* on the clock, the fans *poured* out of the stands and *tore* down the goalposts.

EXERCISE 6-15

The following sentences contain unnecessary shifts. Revise each sentence so that it is consistent in person, number, and tense.

1. Just as I finished putting up my tent, a grizzly bear comes out of the forest.
2. Students should not expect to do well in college unless you study.
3. The books are arranged on the shelves according to the color of its binding.
4. Any driver who parks illegally will have their permit revoked.
5. I phoned Dr. Warren several times yesterday, but he doesn't answer.
6. People who travel during the snowstorm should expect your flights to be delayed.

Remove unrelated ideas from a sentence. A sentence should concentrate on one main idea and related ideas. Put unrelated ideas in their own sentences or even paragraphs. Eliminate any ideas that are unrelated to your purpose.

POOR: John, who likes to play electric guitar, scored ninety-three on his math final.

BETTER: John likes to play electric guitar.
John scored ninety-three on his math final.

POOR: Madeleine, a champion swimmer, went with Cary to the lecture on Swedish glassblowing, which is still practiced in many of the crystal factories in Scandinavia, and they shared a tuna sandwich that Cary made because he ran out of turkey.

BETTER: Madeleine and Cary went to the lecture on Swedish glassblowing, which is still practiced in many of the crystal factories in Scandinavia.

In the latter example, ideas unrelated to glassblowing have been eliminated.

EXERCISE 6-16

Rewrite any of the following sentences that need it, placing unrelated ideas in separate sentences.

1. The dancer, who ate granola and honey every morning for breakfast, had a torn Achilles tendon.
2. Katie went to an aerobic dancing class and played squash to keep in shape.
3. An expert chess player, Bill bought a lottery ticket, won a million dollars, and moved to a mansion in Palm Beach.
4. Pam saw the movie about silver mining and, when she went outside, found a quarter.
5. Teri is an accomplished cook, and she wants to be a veterinarian.
6. The speaker, who started his remarks with a joke, talked about stress in our complex world and then answered questions.

Professional tip. When a sentence is really unclear and you have trouble revising it, look away and say, "What I really mean is. . . ." Then rephrase the sentence as you would speak it. Write those words down. Then substitute your new sentence for the original sentence, and refine the new sentence as necessary.

Here's an example:

UNCLEAR: Regarding grades, studying is the key and I know that I have to work at them if I am going to improve.

WHAT I REALLY
MEAN IS . . .:   I've got to study more if I'm going to get good grades.
REFINED: To get good grades, I have to study more.

✔ Is each sentence concise?

Sentences should be concise—that is, no longer than they need to be. Needless words tax your reader's patience and attention.

How can you judge whether a sentence is concise? Look for words and phrases that add little or nothing to meaning. If all the words contribute to the sentence, it is concise—even if it is long. Which of these sentences is more concise?

> At twelve noon the picketers on strike signed their names at the bottom of the petition.
>
> Heart pounding, eyelids fluttering, and sweat dripping down my forehead, I forced my mouth open and let the dentist drill my molar.

The second sentence is more concise, because every word contributes to its meaning. Over half the words in the first sentence are unnecessary. Noon *is* twelve. The picketers are obviously on strike. Of course they signed their names; what else would they sign? And it doesn't really matter where they signed the petition. Here's a trimmed-down version:

> At noon the picketers signed the petition.

If each sentence is not concise:
Eliminate needless repetition. Weed out redundant words. (If you repeat something for emphasis, that's another thing.) Here are some examples of repetitive phrases:

absolutely complete	end result	intents and purposes
adequate enough	exact same	one and the same
advance planning	exceptionally unique	period of time
all in all	final outcome	personal opinion
ask the question	firm belief	repeat again
attached together	first and foremost	return again
circle around	follow after	the reason is because
consensus of opinion	free gift	thank you kindly
cooperate together	future plans	total effect
disappear from	handsome in	two A.M. in the
sight	appearance	morning
each and every	here and now	various different

EXERCISE 6-17

Remove the unnecessary words from each repetitive phrase in the preceding list.

EXERCISE 6-18

Write down at least five other common examples of needless repetition. Compare your list with those of your classmates.

Don't carelessly repeat words in a sentence. Either cut out the needless words or replace them.

POOR: I am going to *treat* you to a special treat.
BETTER: I am going to give you a treat.
     or
     I am going to treat you to a _____.

POOR: Kim has tried to lose weight often and she often diets.
BETTER: Kim often diets.

EXERCISE 6-19

Revise the following sentences to remove the needless words.

1. Amy will add an additional number of songs.
2. Now that I have showered, I am now ready.
3. For you to join the club, you have to write down the reasons why you want to join the club.
4. My favorite video game is Pac-Man because the game of Pac-Man has a sense of humor.
5. When we actually weighed the weight, the weight weighed more than we expected it to weigh before we weighed it.

Avoid unnecessary introductory phrases. Many introductory phrases are like an elaborate windup before a simple throw. Watch especially for "It. . ." and "There. . ." constructions. You can often simplify or remove such introductions, and go straight to the subject of the sentence without losing any of the meaning. For example:

There are reasons to believe that it will be a nice day.
It should be a nice day.

It would be appreciated if you would milk the cow at sunrise.
Please milk the cow at sunrise.

It seems quite likely that your theory of holiday depression is correct.
Your theory of holiday depression is probably correct.

EXERCISE 6-20

Remove unnecessary introductory phrases from each of the following sentences. Rewrite the sentence if necessary.

1. It is probable that you will get the job.
2. There is no question that the summer doldrums are here.
3. It is a fact that most skin divers look silly in their wet suits.
4. Life being what it is today, we need to study a foreign language.

Shorten wordy prepositional phrases. Usually wordy prepositional phrases can be compressed into one or two words.

During the course of the show, we watched the magician.
During the show we watched the magician.

They climbed the rock face *in a careful manner.*
They climbed the rock face *carefully.*

One prepositional phrase tends to slide into another. You can often cut out most of them without changing a sentence's meaning.

At dusk/in the evening/at the point/in time/at which light meets darkness/I walked home.

I walked home *at dusk.*

As you reread your draft, put prepositional phrases in parentheses or underline them. Later, you can shorten or remove them.

Here are some common wordy prepositional phrases that can be compressed into one or two words. You can probably think of many others.

Wordy	*Concise*
after a while	later
as a matter of fact	actually
as of this date	today, now
due to the fact that	because
in accordance with our request	as requested
in due course of time	eventually
in order to	to
in the event that	if, when
in the not-too-distant future	soon
of the order of magnitude of	approximately, about
on behalf of	for
until such time as	until
with reference to	regarding, about

EXERCISE 6-21

In each of the following sentences, compress or delete the prepositional phrase(s). Make any other necessary changes in sentence structure.

1. The automobile plant is laying off over a hundred workers in view of the fact that sales of the new models have been poor.
2. Break the glass and pull the handle for the purpose of sounding the alarm.
3. Please send us a check in the amount of fifteen dollars.
4. In due course every television set will have a built-in computer.
5. Inasmuch as there is no further business to transact, this meeting is adjourned until such time as another meeting is required.

✔ **Is each sentence vigorous?**

If you want to keep your readers' interest, give your sentences energy and life.

If each sentence is not vigorous:

Avoid "smothered" verbs. The most vigorous way to express action is with an action verb. Yet many writers habitually "smother" their action verbs by turning them into nouns with weak general verbs. Here are some examples:

The committee *held a discussion* of the problem.
CARE *gave help* to the starving refugees.
We must *take action.*

Each of these sentences can be made more direct and concise by "unsmothering" the verb to make it the action verb of the sentence.

> The committee *discussed* the problem.
> CARE *helped* the starving refugees.
> We must *act*.

Check each sentence to find out what its main action is. If the action isn't expressed in the verb, look for a noun that is actually a smothered verb. Such nouns usually end in:

-ion   -ance   -ancy   -ization
-tion   -ence   -ency   -ment

They usually appear with vague, general verbs such as:

make   have   hold   give

EXERCISE 6-22

What verbs are smothered in the following nouns?

1. authorization
2. assessment
3. illustration
4. advancement
5. transmittal
6. documentation
7. concession
8. administration
9. implementation
10. confrontation
11. negotiation
12. determination

EXERCISE 6-23

Improve the following sentences by unsmothering the action verb.

1. The committee reached a decision to fire the dean.
2. The college has a requirement that students write clearly.
3. A club should give consideration to the needs of its members.
4. My sister will make arrangements for the surprise party.
5. Will we hold a meeting tomorrow?
6. The Music Department will give a performance of Handel's *Messiah*.
7. She will make an adjustment in the thermostat.

Check for the passive voice. When a sentence has an action verb, you some- times have to choose between the active voice and the passive voice. In the active voice, the subject of the verb is the doer of the action:

He ate the taco.

In the passive voice, the subject of the verb is whatever is acted upon:

The *taco* was eaten by him.

The passive voice often makes sentences longer, less direct, and less vigor- ous than the active voice. However, the passive voice is the best choice when the doer of the action is unknown:

A cure for dandruff has been found.

rather than

A researcher has found a cure for dandruff.

Or use the passive voice if the doer of the action is less important than the receiver.

The *rock star* was hit by an egg.

rather than

An *egg* hit the rock star.

Don't shift back and forth from active to passive voice without good rea- son. Here's a sentence that shifts for a good reason:

He walked around the corner and was knocked over by a runaway horse.

In this example, the point of view remains consistent because *he* is the sub- ject of both the active verb *walked* and the passive verb *was knocked over.* But in the following sentence, the shift from active to passive voice is also a shift in point of view:

He drove through the red light, and she was nearly run over by him.

Shifts like this can be fixed by changing the passive construction to the ac- tive:

He drove through the red light and nearly ran over her.

EXERCISE 6-24

In the following sentences, change the passive-voice verbs to the active voice, except in cases where the passive voice seems to do the better job.

1. It is recommended by this college that you take a writing course.
2. The election returns were tabulated by representatives of both parties.
3. An essay every week is assigned by my composition instructor.
4. A touchdown pass was blocked by the tackle.
5. A demand was made by the stage manager that the comedian leave the stage.
6. A low-calorie lunch was prepared by my husband.
7. Ms. Grant's assistant was fired by her.
8. The reasons for your resignation have been studied by me, and I agree with them.
9. My first kiss will always be remembered by me.
10. This product has been tested for two years.

EXERCISE 6-25

The following sentences are neither concise nor vigorous. For each sentence, explain why. Then, without changing meanings or simplifying ideas, improve the sentences.

1. In most cases, autobiographies should be written in the first-person singular, using *I* as the subject, although there may be exceptions to this.
2. It was known that they all came to a consensus of opinion in reference to the belief that the abandonment of the run-down urban slums of the inner city to decay and crime is poor enactment of policy on the part of the government at the local, state, and federal levels.
3. In very rare cases, if at all, do members of conservative types of political groups give any degree of approval for the widespread, far-reaching phenomenon of federally funded school lunch programs.
4. During the time that the four young teenagers were waiting for their friends to make their entrance into the dormitory, they shared participation in the mysterious and strange game known throughout the

United States as "D & D" but which is titled in full, "Dungeons and Dragons."

5. Please notice that this example is not included in the research papers that go to make up the enclosure that is included.

✓ **Are the sentences varied in length and structure?**

If not:

Vary sentence length. If all your sentences are the same length, your reader will be bored. Long sentences can connect related information or state complex ideas:

> When the sky turns pink and the snow looks like cotton candy, I like to throw another log on the fire, curl up in a chair, and enjoy winter—at least for an hour or two.

Short sentences, on the other hand, have punch. They emphasize ideas. They add drama. They give the reader a welcome break from complicated sentences. Short sentences are effective in a series, after an especially long sentence, or as a single-word question or answer.

> She wondered if I had enjoyed the trip, if I had seen my old friends, and if I had talked to the old man who had lived next door. I had.

EXERCISE 6-26

In a magazine, newspaper, or textbook, find five paragraphs containing sentences of varied lengths. What is the effect?

Vary sentence structure. Sentences have different kinds of structure. Like sentences of a similar length, sentences all structured the same are likely to bore your reader. By varying the structure of your sentences, you make your writing more interesting.

A *simple sentence* has one independent clause that can stand alone. Each of the following is a simple sentence.

> I got out the tools. I jacked up the car. I changed the flat tire.

A *compound sentence* has at least two independent clauses connected by a conjunction.

I got out the tools, I jacked up the car, and I changed the flat tire.

   independent   independent   independent

A *complex sentence* has one independent clause and at least one dependent clause.

After I got out the tools and jacked up the car, I changed the flat tire.

           dependent   independent

A *compound-complex sentence* has at least two independent clauses and at least one dependent clause.

After I got out the tools, I jacked up the car and I changed the flat tire.

     dependent   independent   independent

✔ Are the sentences structured to provide appropriate emphasis?
If not:

Use sentence structure to emphasize ideas. A series of simple sentences does not show the relative importance of ideas.

He liked the candy. He bought it. He ate it.

When you combine the sentences into a compound sentence, you clearly show that the ideas in each of the independent clauses are of approximately equal importance.

He liked the candy, he bought it, and he ate it.

A complex sentence shows the relative importance of ideas by putting the idea to be emphasized in the independent clause. The idea in the dependent clause is less important and receives less emphasis.

Because he liked the candy, he bought it.

       dependent   independent

After he bought the candy, he ate it.

       dependent   independent

In a compound-complex sentence, the ideas in the independent clauses receive approximately equal emphasis. The less important idea is contained in the dependent clause, where it receives less emphasis.

Because he liked the candy, he bought it, and he ate it.

     dependent   independent   independent

EXERCISE 6-27

The following paragraph is made up of simple sentences, all having the same structure and similar length. Combine some of them into compound, complex, and compound-complex sentences to create greater variety and emphasis.

    A horse race offers many pleasures. You are in the midst of a happy, hopeful crowd. There is the spectacle of the paddock. The jockeys warm up the horses there. The race itself is beautiful. The horses run with speed and grace. There is even more pleasure if your horse wins. But many people don't gamble. They just enjoy the event.

Arrange ideas within sentences for emphasis. The beginning and the ending—especially the ending—are the most emphatic positions in a sentence. Knowing this, you can arrange your sentence so that the main idea is in one of these positions.

In a *loose sentence*, the main idea comes first. Modifying details or other elements are loosely grouped at the end.

> *Sean is going to the doctor* so that he can have his stitches removed before the baseball game next Thursday.

A *periodic sentence* emphasizes the main idea by delaying it until the end.

> Despite the rain, the traffic, and a flat tire along the way, *the trip took only two hours.*

Loose sentences are more common than periodic sentences because beginning with the main idea is a natural way of thinking. Periodic sentences, however, are often more emphatic. To gain emphasis, you may sometimes want to change a loose sentence into a periodic sentence.

LOOSE: The film was not a financial success even though critics unanimously praised it.

PERIODIC: Even though critics unanimously praised it, the film was not a financial success.

EXERCISE 6-28

Rewrite the following sentences in a periodic pattern, according to what you want to emphasize.

1. Fred enjoyed playing backgammon, although he didn't like chess.
2. Joe was the best athlete of all the students in his dorm.
3. Beatrice Sunshine graduated from college at the age of seventy-two.
4. The keyboard, of the approximately eight thousand parts to a piano, is the most frustrating part.
5. The secretary answered yes when I asked if I got the raise.

Use parallelism to gain emphasis. In a parallel sentence, parts that are alike in function are alike in grammatical form.

> Neil likes to eat out, to go to the movies, and to travel.

In this sentence, *to eat, to go,* and *to travel* are parallel elements: each tells us something Neil likes to do. What if the sentence had not been written with a parallel construction?

> Neil likes to eat out, to go to the movies, and traveling.

This sentence is disjointed and distracting.

Parallelism creates an effect of balance and smoothness, but it can also be used to achieve emphasis. By arranging parallel elements in a series in the order of their increasing importance, you emphasize the last and most important element.

UNEMPHATIC: As a reward for fifty years of service, Mr. Maxwell received an all-expense-paid trip to Hawaii, a letter from the company president, and a digital watch.

EMPHATIC: As a reward for fifty years of service, Mr. Maxwell received a letter from the company president, a digital watch, and an all-expense-paid trip to Hawaii.

You can also use a series of parallel sentences to form a strong and emphatic paragraph.

> As your governor, I will encourage the growth of industry in the state. I will improve vital public services. I will obtain fiscal assistance from Washington and reduce state income and property taxes. But I can only fulfill these promises if you vote for me on Election Day.

EXERCISE 6-29

Correct any faulty parallelism in the following sentences.

1. I like to hike, to fish, and I also enjoy camping.
2. I folded my clothes, shut the drawer, turned off the light, disliked my neighbor.
3. Mowing the lawn, cutting flowers, pulling weeds, mulching plants, are chores I do in the garden, as well as watering.
4. Hilda liked to spend Friday nights washing her hair and then propping herself up in bed to read a best-seller until she fell asleep.
5. Prewriting is important, as well as to freewrite and rewrite.
6. Because we care, we should give to charities; because we care, we should consider others; we should do these.

EXERCISE 6-30

Correct these sentences according to the rules they discuss. For example:

Don't make smotherizations of verbs.
Don't smother verbs.

1. Usually, the passive voice should not be used.
2. Remember to, whenever possible, especially in long sentences, not split related parts of a sentence.
3. Check carefully to see if you any words out.
4. If you reread your work, you will find that on rereading a great deal of repetition can be avoided by rereading and correcting.
5. Don't use too many contractions if you want a formal tone.
6. Take cognizance of legal jargon (i.e., Latin and pompous verbiage), and hereinafter preclude it to the fullest possible extent.
7. One must carefully refine your writing to eliminate shifts in point of view.
8. Avoid trendy slang locutions that sound flaky, laid back, or old hat.
9. Never ever use repetitive redundancies.
10. Always pick on the correct idiom.
11. If you have a point you want to emphasize, place it at the end of a sentence and not in the middle of a sentence.
12. It's really very definitely important not to overuse qualifiers.

13. Don't use a big word when a diminutive one will do as well.
14. It is not resultful and will not maximize clarity to transform one part of speech to another.
15. Last but not least, avoid clichés like the plague.

MECHANICS

Mechanics are the details that trip you up as you write: grammar, punctuation, and spelling. There's not much choice involved in fixing mechanical mistakes, so you don't have to spend time making decisions. But you do have to be careful refining your draft, looking for mistakes and correcting them.

If you are shaky about the rules of grammar and punctuation, use a handbook of grammar and usage to help you spot errors and find out how to correct them. If you need spelling help, consult your dictionary.

Most writers make at least a few grammatical errors in a draft. Common errors include the sentence fragment, the run-on sentence, the comma splice, subject-verb agreement, and dangling words and phrases.

✔ **Are your sentences grammatically correct?**
If not:
Avoid sentence fragments. A sentence fragment is a word or group of words punctuated as if it were a sentence, even though it isn't. Correct a fragment by making it into a complete sentence or joining it to another sentence nearby.

FRAGMENT: The ground shaking with tremors. (*no verb*)
CORRECTED: The ground was shaking with tremors.

FRAGMENT: She came to the housewarming party. Though she didn't want to. (*dependent clause without main clause*)
CORRECTED: She came to the housewarming party though she didn't want to.

FRAGMENT: Tumbling into the pool, making a splash that soaked everyone within twenty feet. (*no subject or verb*)
CORRECTED: Tumbling into the pool, Jimmy made a splash that soaked everyone within twenty feet.

One kind of practical writing—advertising—uses many sentence fragments. Some writers purposely use sentence fragments to create an informal quality or to create emphasis. But even these kinds of sentence fragment can be irritating, so it's best to avoid them.

EXERCISE 6-31

Convert the following sentence fragments into complete sentences.

1. A dream: to write a novel.
2. Because Chinese food is cheap.
3. Registration time, filled with anticipation and long lines.
4. Fish, the easiest pets to care for.
5. The *New York Times* motto: "All the news that's fit to print."
6. The smell of rolls drifting through the bakery.

Avoid run-on sentences. A run-on sentence is two or more independent clauses connected without any punctuation. Correct a run-on sentence by making separate sentences or by using semicolons or by using a comma and a conjunction such as *and, but, or, for, yet,* and *so.*

INCORRECT: My sister always tickles me I hate it.
CORRECT: My sister always tickles me. I hate it.
           or
           My sister always tickles me; I hate it.
           or
           My sister always tickles me, but I hate it.

Avoid comma splice. A comma splice occurs when two independent clauses are joined with only a comma. Correct a comma splice by replacing the comma with a period or semicolon or by adding a conjunction following the comma.

INCORRECT: When I ask her to stop, she ignores me, then she tickles me harder.
CORRECT: When I ask her to stop, she ignores me. Then she tickles me harder.
           or
           When I ask her to stop, she ignores me; then she tickles me harder.
           or
           When I ask her to stop she ignores me and then she tickles me harder.

EXERCISE 6-32

Indicate whether each of the following is a comma splice or a run-on sentence by marking it *C* or *R*. Then correct the punctuation.

1. The runner put every bit of his energy into the race as he crossed the finish line the crowd roared.

2. The weather was clear, everything was going well on the canoe trip so far.
3. They went out on their first date together, they said they would go out again soon.
4. Toads are ugly frogs are not as muddy-looking.
5. Many alternate ways of financing a home are now available high interest rates have made that necessary.

Check that the subject and verb agree. Don't be fooled by nouns in prepositional phrases that come between the subject and the verb and differ in number from the subject. It is the number—singular or plural—of the subject only that determines the number of the verb.

INCORRECT: The *need* for this summer job and others like it *are* strong.
CORRECT: The *need* for this summer job and others like it *is* strong.

INCORRECT: The *consequences* of the valve sticking *is* apparent.
CORRECT: The *consequences* of the valve sticking *are* apparent.

EXERCISE 6-33

Correct any of the following sentences in which the subjects and verbs do not agree.

1. The smallest one of the begonias need special attention.
2. Neither heat nor cold is comfortable.
3. In this kit is the directions.
4. The commander as well as his associates were at the reception.
5. The last of the drinks are on the table.
6. *Sons and Lovers* are an important novel.

Check that modifying phrases don't dangle. A modifying phrase without a subject dangles out in front of a sentence without any clear relationship to the other parts. For example:

Pouring rain, we cancelled the game.
Although only a child, my mother took me to Europe.

To correct a dangling modifier, rearrange the words so the modifier clearly relates to the words it should modify. Or add words to make the meaning clearer.

Because it was pouring rain, we cancelled the game.
Although I was only a child, my mother took me to Europe.
or
Although only a child, I accompanied my mother to Europe.

EXERCISE 6-34

Revise the following sentences to correct the dangling modifiers.

1. Falling apart, he paid only ten dollars for the chair.
2. Pondering the problem, his head fell on the pillow.
3. When a little girl, my grandaunt made me gingerbread cookies.
4. As a good writer, my pencil is always rewriting.
5. Although asked if it was true, not an answer was given.

✔ Are the punctuation and capitalization correct?

Punctuation and capitalization help clarify your writing. Everybody knows that each sentence must start with a capital letter and end with a period, that other punctuation marks set off some grammatical divisions within sentences, and that all proper nouns and adjectives begin with a capital letter. However, many writers have problems with various uses of punctuation. You should always reread your draft assuming that some of the capitalization and punctuation may be wrong.

If the punctuation and capitalization are not correct:

Consult a handbook of grammar and usage. If a punctuation mark in your draft looks wrong or you're not sure whether to capitalize a certain word, circle it; then consult a handbook to determine the correct usage.

Keep a list of frequent errors.

✔ Are all the words spelled correctly?

If not:

Look up the word(s) in your dictionary. If you're even a little bit doubtful that you've spelled a word correctly, look it up. The half a minute you spend is insurance against being wrong.

Professional tip. Discovering errors in your own writing can be difficult. If you'd known they were mistakes, you wouldn't have made them. Thus, it's a good idea to ask someone you trust—perhaps your instructor—to point out the errors in your draft. He or she shouldn't correct them, however—that's for you to do.

SUMMARY

In Step Six—refine—you should:

- Reread your draft carefully and objectively, looking for problems in general style, word choice, sentence style and structure, and mechanics.
- Mark problems with a colored pencil, using symbols if you wish. Make notes to yourself on the draft for solving the problems.
- Ask yourself the following questions:
    - ✔ Is the style right for your topic, purpose, and readers?
    - ✔ Is the tone right for your topic, purpose, and readers?
    - ✔ Are the style and tone consistent?
    - ✔ Is each word used precisely?
    - ✔ Is each word specific?
    - ✔ Are the words appropriate?
    - ✔ Are the words fresh?
    - ✔ Is each sentence clear?
    - ✔ Is each sentence concise?
    - ✔ Is each sentence vigorous?
    - ✔ Are the sentences varied in length and structure?
    - ✔ Are the sentences structured to provide appropriate emphasis?
    - ✔ Are the grammar, punctuation, capitalization, and spelling correct?
- Make changes in the draft according to your answers to these questions and your penciled notes on the draft.

Neatness counts.

Step 7: Recopy

By now, you should have a sense of accomplishment, because you are about to complete a successful piece of writing. You've already done the hard part. You have only one last step: recopying your draft into final form.

BE NEAT

One of the goals of good writing is clarity not only in meaning but also in presentation. Handwriting is often difficult to read. So if you must write your final paper in longhand, be sure to write legibly.

If you can type the paper, do so. The typewriter should have all characters working and a fresh ribbon. If you don't have a typewriter, perhaps you can borrow or rent one. And if you can't type, consider trading skills with someone who can. Or hire a typist.

If you have made some corrections on the final draft, use your judgment about whether you should recopy all or parts of it to make it neater. With a research paper that will determine your final grade for a course, you probably should.

FOLLOW A FORMAT

Before recopying, decide on details such as margins, pagination, captions, lists, address blocks, salutations, and closings. Your instructor may suggest a format for you to use, or you may want to create your own. Here are some suggestions.

For typewritten papers, use regular 8½-by-11-inch white bond paper. Be sure to leave margins of at least 1 inch at the top, bottom, and sides of each page. Type on one side of each sheet, and double-space between the lines. Indent each new paragraph. Number each page in the upper right-hand corner.

For any long or important paper or report, provide a title page. Center the title and your name on the upper half of the page. Near the bottom you may want to include other identifying information, such as course name and number, instructor's name, assignment number, and date submitted.

For handwritten pages, the format is essentially the same. Use 8½-by-11-inch lined notebook paper, and double-space between lines. Write in black or blue ink.

Put appendices, indexes, and visuals in the proper place. And if you've quoted from sources, use footnotes and a bibliography; see pages 155–165.

PROOFREAD

When you've recopied your paper, check it carefully for careless copying mistakes and typographical errors. A copying mistake might be a word, sentence, or page written twice. It could be the omission of a key word or chapter. If you meant to state "and so the evidence shows that the proposed solution is not feasible" and left out *not*, the consequences could be devastating.

Some other areas prone to recopying errors include:

spelling
days/dates
names
spacing of words
running paragraphs together
breaking a paragraph into two
incorrect placement of visuals or captions
incorrect page numbering

Recopying errors may be hard to find, because *you* made them. Writers often repeat spelling, punctuation, and grammar mistakes without recognizing them. So, if possible, have someone else proofread your writing. With lists of numbers or statistics, you can read them aloud while your reader checks the copy.

Finally, proofread your paper by yourself. Go line by line, word by word, punctuation mark by punctuation mark, making sure that each element in the draft has been transferred correctly to the final copy.

Use symbols to add missing letters or words (see page 98); you can use correction fluid to delete extra words or letters. Small adjustments, neatly made, are usually acceptable on the final copy. But when corrections are numerous enough to distract the reader, recopy the page.

As you proofread, you may discover flaws or omissions in organization, content, style, tone, or detail that you didn't notice in the draft. This often creates a dilemma. For example, after writing about "The Forgotten Vietnam Veteran," you now read in the paper that Congress has approved new benefits for these veterans. This new fact doesn't support your controlling idea. Using it will mean rewriting and retyping at least a page. But you know it's important. Should you add it? Yes! The extra time you spend will be worth it for you and for your reader.

EXERCISE 7-1

Proofread the following paragraph, correcting any error you find.

Are you intrested in staying at 1 of the nicest places in america. Sea winds is one of premeir sports complexes in the country. The resorts recreational amenitys include, two Championship golf course, 60 tennis courts, 6 miles of ocenfront beAch, 20 miles of bike trails and 6 pools. Thier are also riding stabiles, fishing boats and sail boats, as as well as miles of jogging and walking trails. For those less sports minded their is indoor recretion includeing video games, and activities like danceing and singalongs.

SUMMARY

In Step Seven—recopy—you should:

- Be neat.
- Follow a format.
- Proofread.

You've now finished the seven steps to better writing. Remember the wobbly feeling you had the first time you tried to ride a bike? The more you rode, the less you wobbled. Eventually, perhaps you didn't even hold onto the handlebars. You can do the same with writing. Follow the steps. Keep at it. The more you write, the better you'll get. And remember the old joke about the tourist in New York City who stopped a man to ask for directions.

"Excuse me, sir," the tourist said. "How do I get to the Metropolitan Opera?"

"Only one way," answered the man. "Practice."

Knowledge is of two kinds. We know a subject ourselves, or we know where we can find information about it.

SAMUEL JOHNSON

The Research Paper

It would be wonderful if you knew everything you needed to know for your practical writing. Of course, that's not possible. That's why there are libraries and so many people using them to find things out.

Sometimes you go to the library to verify information, to back up your personal experiences and observations. Even if all you do is look up the capital of Albania or find out which states have citizen revolts against high taxes, that's library research.

Many papers you write in college will take you outside that which you know from experience and observation or remember from earlier studies. Suppose your American government professor requires you to write about "Corruption in Government." You recall that the mayor of your hometown lost an election because of a bribery scandal, and you probably remember something about Watergate. But memories are not enough for a research paper. To do the job well, you will have to gather information from books, magazines, and newspapers in the library.

Except for the way you gather information, writing a research paper is much like other kinds of practical writing. It involves the same seven steps.

Here's an outline of the steps that includes the special requirements for doing a research paper:

Step One: Choose a topic.
Step Two: Gather information
  Use the library.
  Plan.
      Determine kinds of sources.
      Find sources.
      List and evaluate sources.
      Read and take notes.
Step Three: Organize
Step Four: Write a draft.
  Quotations.
  Paraphrase.
  Summary.
Step Five: Revise.
Step Six: Refine.
Step Seven: Recopy.
  Add footnotes.
  Add the bibliography.
  Determine format for bibliography and footnotes.
  Determine the final format.

This discussion assumes that you have read the rest of the book and know the seven steps for doing practical writing. Here you will find only new information about doing library research and using that research in your writing. If necessary, check back to remind yourself of the procedures and suggestions for the step you're working on.

STEP ONE: CHOOSE A TOPIC

As with any writing project, begin with a manageable topic. For a research project, you need a topic that you can research in a variety of sources. But you must be able to get through the sources in the time available to you.

For example, "Corruption in Government" could occupy months or even years of research. You could write a book about it; many have. You should narrow a topic that broad to one that you can handle within the limitations of your assignment. Get an idea of possible topics from your course textbook or from concise articles in encyclopedias, biographical dictionaries, and other sources. Choose two or three topics you'd like to write about, such as "The Watergate Scandal," and if possible discuss them with the person who will be reading your paper.

If you can, decide on a controlling idea before beginning your research. This may seem difficult, because the gathering and reading of sources lie ahead and you may know relatively little about your topic. But even if you have to change the controlling idea later, it can help you do your research. You will know what kind of sources to look at and what kind of information in them you can use; just as important, you'll know what kind of information to skip over. An example of a controlling idea on Watergate would be "The Watergate scandal was an unprecedented instance of presidential involvement in corrupt activities."

STEP TWO: GATHER INFORMATION

Unlike brainstorming, in which you explore your experiences and observations to discover ideas for your writing, gathering information by research involves detective work. You look for clues to lead you to the sources that will provide the information you need. The clues are in various places in the library—in the card catalog, in indexes to magazines and newspapers, in bibliographies, and in books on your topic. It's up to you to find them.

Plan

Locating sources, reading them, and taking notes are part of Step Two. Writing the paper from your notes is similar to using your own ideas; however, there are some important differences. You can't change what your sources say the way you can change your own opinion, and you must identify in your paper where each piece of information came from.

There's also another difference. In brainstorming, you should free yourself to think about anything that is connected with your topic. Later you can choose the most important and useful ideas, and discard the rest. But in library research, if you tried to read everything about your topic, you would never finish. So your most important job in planning a research paper is to list the sources you absolutely must read. From these, you should be able to gather all the information you need:

Use the Library

Finding a book when you know its author and title isn't hard—you just look it up in the card catalog, find its call number, go to the stacks, and the book is in your hands. In library research, however, you're looking for books, periodicals, and other sources that will help you, whether you know their titles and authors or not.

To track down sources, you have to know what sources the library has and where they're kept. If there is an orientation tour available, take it, and ask questions relating to your research project. If the stacks are open, browse through the books on your topic. If the stacks are closed, try to get a stacks pass. Read any pamphlets that the library has published explaining its organization and research facilities.

Be sure to introduce yourself to the reference librarian, who can help you both find reference materials and plan your research. Librarians won't do the research for you, but they can help you get started.

DETERMINE KINDS OF SOURCES

To compile a working bibliography, you have to know something about the different kinds of sources and about where to locate books on your topic.

There are two main kinds of sources: primary and secondary. A primary source is an original, firsthand document; a secondary source is any document based on a primary source. A secondary source compiles or interprets information from primary sources or provides background for them. For example, a literary work is a primary source; literary criticism and biography are secondary sources. (They may help you understand and appreciate a primary work, but they aren't a substitute for reading it.) Albert Einstein's 1905 paper on relativity is a primary source; a popularized explanation of it is a secondary source. An eyewitness account of a bank robbery is a primary source; a report in a newspaper or a history book is secondary.

You can and should use both types of sources. A primary source such as an autobiography may not tell the unvarnished truth; secondary sources may keep you from being taken in. However, a secondary source is always a selection and an interpretation. If you go to the primary sources yourself, you can make your own selection and interpretation.

Reference Books. Reference books are secondary sources. Some are kept in the reference room of a library; others are kept in the stacks. Use *general encyclopedias* to verify information. Some have indexes in case you don't know under which subject the information you want is located.

There are also *specialized encyclopedias* and *dictionaries* for many fields, ranging from biography to music and literature to chemistry and engineering. The more specialized a reference book, the more detailed and technical it will probably be.

If you have to find information too recent to be in an encyclopedia, try *almanacs* and *yearbooks.* If the information is still more recent, try the *New York Times Index* for news stories and the *Readers' Guide to Periodical Literature* for magazine articles.

Books. Except for works of literature, autobiographies, and some original research in the social sciences, most books are secondary sources. They are kept in the stacks, arranged by subject. They range from serious, scholarly works based on solid research and documented by footnotes, to fluffy, popularized exploitations of little research value. Try to use the most accurate and well-reasoned sources available for your topic. (On pages 147–148, you will find some tips on evaluating sources.)

Periodicals. Articles in magazines, scholarly journals, and newspapers are sometimes primary sources, sometimes secondary. For example, nearly all original scientific work is published in journal articles, rather than in books. Like books, articles must be evaluated for accuracy and usefulness. Current issues of periodicals are usually kept in the periodical room. Back issues are bound and kept either on shelves in the periodical room or in the stacks, arranged by title. Some periodicals, especially newspapers, are not bound but instead are transferred to microfilm or microfiche.

Other Sources. Many libraries have collections of sound recordings, films, videodisks, videotapes, and art reproductions. Ask the librarian where you can find a catalog of these holdings.

FIND SOURCES

The key to finding relevant sources is to work with your topic. Books are classified and cataloged by subject; periodicals are indexed by subject; reference books are organized by subject. Be sure to consider all subject classifications that may include the information you are looking for.

Books. Use the subject cards in the card catalog. If you were looking for books on the Watergate scandal, you would find them under the subject heading "Watergate Affair, 1972- ," which is typed across the top. On the next line is the call number, which helps you to locate the book on the library's shelves.

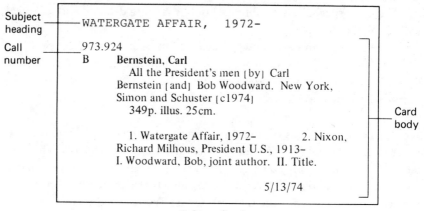

Subject heading ————WATERGATE AFFAIR,   1972–

Call number
973.924
B   Bernstein, Carl
           All the President's men [by] Carl
        Bernstein [and] Bob Woodward. New York,
        Simon and Schuster [c1974]
           349p. illus. 25cm.

           1. Watergate Affair, 1972–   2. Nixon,
        Richard Milhous, President U.S., 1913–
        I. Woodward, Bob, joint author. II. Title.

                              5/13/74

Card body

Subject Card

Also look for bibliographies in the magazines, books, and encyclopedias you consult. If any titles look promising, search for them under their authors' names in the card catalog.

Periodicals. The card catalog lists the titles of the periodicals the library keeps, and the years it has kept them. It does not give the contents of the individual issues. Use one of the periodical indexes, which list articles according to subject area. The major indexes are:

Readers' Guide to Periodical Literature: indexes popular, large-circulation magazines.

Humanities Index: indexes periodicals specializing in archaeology, classical studies, area studies, folklore, history, language and literature, literary and political criticism, performing arts, philosophy, religion, and theology.

Social Sciences Index: indexes periodicals specializing in anthropology, area studies, economics, environmental science, education, law and criminology, medical science, political science, psychology, public administration, and sociology. (The *Humanities Index* and the *Social Sciences Index* were published in combined form from 1907 to 1965 as the

International Index, and from 1965 to 1974 as the *Social Sciences and Humanities Index.*)

New York Times Index: indexes all news stories, articles, editorials, book reviews, and other materials that have appeared in the *New York Times.* You can also use it as a partial index to other newspapers by checking the date when a particular event was reported in the *Times.*

There are also specialized periodical indexes to fields in the humanities, social sciences, and natural sciences, such as *Applied Science and Technology Index, Art Index, Business Periodicals Index, Education Index,* and *Music Index.* These indexes are usually kept in the periodical room or the reference room; the reference librarian will help you in your search.

In the sciences, published papers are not only indexed but summarized very briefly in sources such as *Biological Abstracts, Chemical Abstracts, Psychological Abstracts,* and *Sociological Abstracts.* Reading the abstract can help you decide whether the article is relevant to your topic and should be included in your working bibliography.

LIST AND EVALUATE SOURCES

Save yourself time and trouble by including only potentially useful sources in your list. For a ten-page research paper, you'll need a variety of sources (books and journal articles), some of which you'll discard. A shorter paper requires fewer sources. Eliminate:

- *Irrelevant sources.* If you are writing about a topic that deals with the Great Depression, you'll find hundreds of books and articles about the period. Some are general overviews; others deal with specific economic, social, or cultural happenings or trends. Don't bother to list sources that have little or nothing to do with your specific topic. For example, if you're writing about the crisis of bank closings, an article about printing currency will be irrelevant.
- *Outdated sources.* Particularly in the natural sciences, but also in fields such as economics and political science, knowledge and theory can advance so fast that books often become obsolete. Sometimes the publication date will tell you whether or not a book is obsolete, but often you won't discover this until you start reading.
- *Duplicate sources.* Books that are general overviews of their subjects— for example, college textbooks—are often very similar in their coverage and point of view. Keep the number of such books on your source

list down to three or four, and try to make the most of sources that focus specifically on your topic.

- *Popular sources.* Popular sources include books and magazine articles written to simplify complex ideas and information for mass circulation. For the most part, they rehash the more serious, scholarly work that you should be reading. You may find popular sources helpful in understanding an unfamiliar topic, but try not to depend on them as your main sources of information.

Sometimes, no matter how choosy you are, your list of possible sources becomes too long, and you don't have time to read them all. If this happens, your topic is probably still too broad. Look at the sources you've listed. Do their titles suggest a narrower topic that you can handle in the available time? If so, discuss the new topic with your instructor or reader.

For example, Watergate would be much too broad a topic for a term paper. You would find hundreds of newspaper and magazine articles and quite a few books devoted to some aspect of Watergate. Perhaps you're interested in precisely what the president himself did that was corrupt. Your new topic might be "Presidential Wrongdoing in the Watergate Scandal." Of course, if you change your focus, you also have to change your controlling idea: for instance, "Richard Nixon committed corrupt acts as president that justified his being driven from office."

Although you now have a list of sources, you're not quite ready to start taking detailed notes. First, you must evaluate whether your sources are useful and sufficient.

Skim all your sources. Read through them quickly if they're about your topic, or if they're broader, look up your topic in the table of contents or index.

Look at the footnotes and bibliographies of your sources for titles of other books and articles about the topic. Add any promising titles to your list, and check to see whether they are available.

What if your library doesn't have an important source? You might be able to find it in a nearby library. If not, the librarian can often arrange an interlibrary loan. However, such a loan can take several weeks, so start your research early.

READ AND TAKE NOTES

As you read your sources, look for information and opinions that support or oppose your controlling idea—the point you want to make. Exclude irrelevant facts or observations, however interesting they may be.

You can take three kinds of notes from a source:

- *Quotations.* Sometimes, when the exact words in a source are especially memorable or important, you may decide to quote the source directly. Occasionally, there may be no other way to describe something—for example, a chemical process. When you have to quote, make sure you do so exactly, with no changes in wording or punctuation. Here is an example:

  > "And let us begin by committing ourselves to the truth, to see it like it is, to tell it like it is—to find the truth, to speak the truth and to live the truth—and that's what we will do."

- *Paraphrase.* Whenever you don't have to quote, *paraphrase*; that is, take your notes in your own words. Don't just substitute synonyms in the original sentence structure; rather, find your own way of stating what the source says. Below, the first paraphrase keeps too many of the source's words; the second paraphrase is better.

  > In 1968, President Nixon committed his administration to finding, speaking, and living the truth, promising that that is what it would do.

  > In 1968, President Nixon pledged that his administration would discover, tell, and act on the truth.

- *Summary.* Unlike a quotation or a paraphrase, a summary does not reproduce all the details of a source. Rather, it uses the main idea and key points in a brief account of the original. For example, a plot summary of a novel might take a few pages; an abstract of a scientific article is usually a short paragraph.

  Here is a summary of the Nixon quotation:

  > In 1968, President Nixon pledged that his administration would be truthful.

As you read your sources, take notes that paraphrase or summarize any information or opinion that relates to your controlling idea. In addition, write down any important quotations. After you've finished reading, summarize the book or article. The summary will help refresh your memory when you are writing your paper, and sometimes you can use it directly in your paper.

The most convenient format for note-taking is a four- by six-inch or five-by seven-inch index card, either lined or plain. It's big enough to hold a fair amount of information, yet small enough to force you to be selective in paraphrasing and concise in summarizing.

Put each quotation, paraphrase, or summary on a separate card. Later, you can arrange the cards in the sequence you want your paper to follow. Write your note on one side of the card, leaving about three quarters of an inch blank at the top. Enter the page number(s) of the source in the upper right-hand corner. In the upper left-hand corner, write the author's last name, the title of the publication, and the year of the publication. (If a source doesn't have an author or editor, list the title first, as shown on the sample note card.) If two or more sources have the same author and year, mark the first one *a*, the next one *b*, etc. If possible, decide on a subject heading for each note card, and put it at the bottom of the card. This will help you later when you organize your paper.

Note card

Bibliography card

Before putting your source aside, make a bibliography card for it—a card containing all the information needed to list it correctly in your bibliography. Use three- by five-inch cards to distinguish them from note cards. To save time and trouble, write the bibliography card in the format you will use in the bibliography. (Examples of bibliography entries for the most common types of sources can be found on pages 157–165.)

STEP THREE: ORGANIZE

If you assigned subject headings to the note cards as you wrote them, you have already begun to organize. If you didn't, do it now. Classify each card according to its content. Then sort the note cards into groups according to related subjects.

You should have five to ten groups, each containing several cards. This indicates that you have read enough to accumulate notes on several important aspects of your topic and that you have classified the notes so that each aspect is completely covered.

What if you have one large pile of note cards and a dozen or so individual cards, each with an unrelated subject heading? Perhaps you classified the cards carelessly. Go through the pile; should some cards be reclassified with narrower subjects? Look at the stragglers. Do some of them also belong in those subjects? Even after careful reconsideration, some cards still may not fit into any of the groups. Set them aside; they are not useful for your controlling idea.

Next, reconsider your controlling idea. You've done a good deal of research. Do the facts and arguments you've found support your controlling idea? Or have you reached new conclusions from your reading? If so, create a new controlling idea that expresses them—for example, "President Nixon's role in the Watergate scandal justified his being driven out of office."

Now copy down the subject headings of the various groups. Treat them in the same way you treated the major ideas in Step Three: select a pattern of development, and write an outline in which the subject headings are arranged according to your developmental pattern. (If necessary, review Step Three.) Frequent patterns used in research papers are:

- *Narration*. Useful in history and biography.
- *Comparison and contrast*. Useful when your sources offer widely differing interpretations and opinions.

- *Argument.* Useful whenever you present evidence and reasoning to support a conclusion.

Feel free to modify the subject headings in order to fit the pattern of development or combination of patterns you have chosen. For example, if you are writing a research paper that compares and contrasts two sides of an argument, you may want to reclassify the note cards so that you can easily see which side of the argument each note supports.

Now arrange the note cards once again so that their sequence matches that of major ideas in the outline. Then look at each individually, and put it in its proper place in the sequence according to the outline.

When you write your rough draft, you must keep clear which ideas and words are your own and which are taken from your sources, so that later you can add footnotes for your source materials. To simplify this, number the note cards. Then, when you use material from note card 1, write "(1)" in the draft where it appears; when you use material from note card 2, write "(2)"; and so on. Also use this system to avoid copying quotations from cards; leave a space where a quotation should go, and write "quote" and the number of the note card in the space—for example, "quote 8." When you revise, insert the full quotation.

As you review the note cards, you may find that two or more of your sources disagree with each other. If they disagree over a matter of fact, such as when somebody died, then you must do more research to discover the correct date. But if they differ over a matter of opinion, then there is no "correct" answer. You have two options: either present the disagreement without taking sides, or support one side. In either case, be sure to include the key points each source makes to support its position.

STEP FOUR: WRITE A DRAFT

Use your notes as if they were your own brainstormed ideas; get them down on paper. If you disagree with a source, feel free to argue your own point of view—or use other sources to argue it for you.

When drafting or revising a research paper, you must fit the paraphrases and summaries from your notes into your own writing without changing their meaning. And quotations must be fit in without changing the words.

Quotations

A source's exact wording and punctuation must be preserved in a quotation. However, you can omit words from a quotation that are not essential to its meaning. Such omissions are indicated with three spaced periods, called *ellipsis points*. (When an ellipsis occurs at the end of a sentence, it is preceded by a period.) Compare the following:

ORIGINAL: "When people are dishonorable in private business, they injure only those with whom they deal or their own chances in the next world. But when there is a lack of honor in government, the morals of the whole people are poisoned."

—Herbert Hoover, 1951

ELLIPSIS: "When people are dishonorable in private business, they injure only those with whom they deal. . . . But when there is a lack of honor in government, the morals of the whole people are poisoned."

IMPROPER ELLIPSIS: "When people are dishonorable in private business. . . the morals of the whole people are poisoned."

Using an ellipsis allows you to omit Hoover's reference to life after death, which isn't relevant to a paper about corruption in government. But be careful. Improper use of an ellipsis can destroy a quotation; in the preceding example, Hoover is quoted as saying the very opposite of what he actually said.

You might decide that Hoover's first sentence is irrelevant to your topic. If you delete it, note the word *But* at the beginning of the second sentence makes no sense and has to go too:

". . . when there is a lack of honor in government, the morals of the whole people are poisoned."

A short quotation—four typewritten lines or less—should appear in the body of your writing set off by quotation marks:

Concern about corruption in government goes back to the earliest years of the American republic. Thomas Jefferson said in 1774, "The whole art of government consists in the art of being honest."

A lengthy quotation should be set off from the rest of the text by indenting it. No quotation marks are needed. For example:

In 1961, President John F. Kennedy also spoke on the subject of corruption in government:
No President can excuse or pardon the slightest deviation from irreproachable standards of behavior on the part of any member of the executive branch. For his firmness and determination is the ultimate source of public confidence in the government of the United States.

Finally, sometimes you need to insert an explanatory word or phrase into a quotation to help readers understand it. Set off any such insertion by using brackets:

> John F. Kennedy insisted that the "firmness and determination [of the president] is the ultimate source of public confidence in the government of the United States."

Don't make more than one insertion into a quotation. If a source requires more than one explanatory insertion, paraphrase it. If you disagree with what a source says, don't use insertions to argue with it. Rather, present your argument after the quotation.

Paraphrase

A paraphrase is handled like an indirect quotation: use no quotation marks. Change the verb tenses inside the paraphrase, if necessary, so that they agree with the tense of the surrounding passage. For example:

> In 1961 President Kennedy said that no president could afford to condone improper conduct among his subordinates, because the people's trust in their government depends upon the chief executive's ethical standards.

Remember, no matter how may times you rewrite a paraphrase, you must still report accurately what the source said. And even though the words and sentence structure may be yours, you must still tell your readers where you found the ideas. Failure to do this is plagiarism.

Summary

Summary is also handled like indirect quotation, without quotation marks and with verb tenses that fit the context. If your notes contain a summary of an entire magazine article, you may want to use only that part which supports a point you are making. For example:

COMPLETE
SUMMARY: Not all public officials are corrupt, but too many are. The American West was won not just by killing Indians but by bribing Congressmen to back expansionist legislation. But public opinion has changed this. Open bribes are clumsy and seem rarer than they were, but citizens should not have too much trust.

Citizens should be vigilant and involved. They should ask questions about their own communities—for example, do corporations choose not to set up businesses there? State laws like Florida's can make public who gave and who received political campaign contributions. Public officials should be required to disclose their finances and obey well-enforced codes of ethics.

—Thomas Griffith (*Time*, 31 December 1973)

SELECTIVE
SUMMARY: At the end of 1973, a year in which the vice president had resigned because of bribery charges and the president's own involvement in Watergate had become obvious, Thomas Griffith recommended in *Time* that state laws like Florida's be enacted that make public who makes political contributions and who receives them. He also argued that public officials be required to disclose their finances and obey well-enforced codes of ethics.

Again, remember that you must give credit to the source you have summarized.

STEP FIVE: REVISE

When writing a research paper, use the checklist on page 79. Now that the material is down on paper, you can concentrate on how smoothly it is organized and whether it focuses on your topic, purpose, and controlling idea.

STEP SIX: REFINE

Follow the checklist on page 101. If you have used material from many sources, make sure that your style and tone are consistent.

STEP SEVEN: RECOPY

In research papers, Step Seven involves adding the notes and bibliography, as well as recopying.

Add Notes

Each time you quote, paraphrase, or summarize a source, include a note identifying it. Although *footnotes* are still used at the foot of the page, *endnotes* at the end of the paper just before the bibliography are more common. In either case, place a superscript number in the paper at the end of the use of the source, beginning with "1" for the first note and continuing with "2" for the second, and so on. For each number in the body of the text, supply a corresponding note. Here's an example:

According to Duane Lockhard, Watergate represented something simultaneously old and new. It was solidly rooted in the great tradition of corruption in American politics. But it was also the first time that some of the dirtiest techniques of the espionage community were adopted in a presidential campaign. [19]

[19] Duane Lockhard, "The 'Great Tradition' of American Corruption," New Society, 31 May 1973, pp. 486-88.

You may use the same source several times in one piece of writing. The first time, give a full note to document the source. For subsequent citations, you can write a much shorter note.

[9] Dwight Waldo, The Enterprise of Public Administration (Novato, Calif.: Chandler and Sharp, 1980), pp. 103-08.

[10] Waldo, pp. 110-12.

Avoid any possible confusion. For example, if you use more than one work by an author, simply citing the author's last name in a later note will leave your reader uncertain which source you are referring to; thus, you must also give the titles.

[18] Waldo, The Enterprise of Public Administration, p. 184.

[19] Waldo, The Administrative State, p. 74.

Add the Bibliography

The bibliography should list any sources from which you took notes or gained information you did not already know. Even if you don't cite a source in your footnotes, you can list it in your bibliography. But do not list sources that added nothing to the understanding of your topic.

The entries in a bibliography should be arranged alphabetically by the author's last name. If there are several sources by the same author, they should be arranged chronologically, in order of publication, or alphabetically, by title. For entries after the first, a row of ten hyphens followed by a period is used to stand for the author's full name in the first entry. If the list contains (1) works by an author alone and (2) works in which the same author has collaborated with others and is named by the source as the main author, the single-authorship entries should come first. The multiple-authorship entries should follow, arranged alphabetically by the last name of the *second* author.

Determine Formats for Bibliography and Notes

The standard style for documenting sources for papers in English courses and for some kinds of practical writing can be found in the *MLA Handbook* (New York: Modern Language Association, 1977). This inexpensive paperback, available in most college libraries and bookstores, shows you how to document many different kinds of sources.

The natural and social sciences do not use the MLA style of documentation. In fact, many professional fields dictate their own style. Ask your instructor or your supervisor which style you should use.

In the following pages, you will find sample bibliography and note entries for the most commonly used kinds of sources. Observe that a bibliography entry is punctuated and indented differently from a note. Also, a note always indicates the page or pages from which you're quoting, paraphrasing, or summarizing.

BOOKS

One author

Bibliography:

Gilson, Lawrence. Money and Secrecy: A Citizen's Guide to Reforming State and Federal Practices. New York: Praeger, 1972.

Note:

[1] Lawrence Gilson, Money and Secrecy: A Citizen's Guide to Reforming State and Federal Practices (New York: Praeger, 1972), p. 62.

More than one author

Bibliography:

Beard, Edmund, and Stephen Horn.   Congressional Ethics: The View
    from the House.   Washington: Brookings Institution, 1975.

Note:

² Edmund Beard and Stephen Horn, Congressional Ethics: The View
from the House (Washington: Brookings Institution, 1975), p. 16.

Anonymous author

Bibliography:

The Federalist.   Ed. Jacob E. Cooke.   New York: Columbia Univ.
    Press, 1961.

Note:

³ The Federalist, ed. Jacob E. Cooke (New York: Columbia
Univ. Press, 1961), pp. 21-22.

Book with an editor

Bibliography:

Martin, Roscoe C., ed.   Public Administration and Democracy:
    Essays in Honor of Paul H. Appleby.   Syracuse: Syracuse
    Univ. Press, 1965.

Note:

⁴ Roscoe C. Martin, ed., Public Administration and Democracy:
Essays in Honor of Paul H. Appleby.   (Syracuse: Syracuse Univ.
Press, 1965), p. 101.

Chapter or other part of a book

Bibliography:

Bailey, Stephen K. "Ethics and the Public Service." In

    Public Administration and Democracy: Essays in Honor

    of Paul H. Appleby. Ed. Roscoe C. Martin. Syracuse:

    Syracuse Univ. Press, 1965, pp. 283-98.

Note:

[5] Stephen K. Bailey, "Ethics and the Public Service," in

Public Administration and Democracy: Essays in Honor of Paul

H. Appleby, ed. Roscoe C. Martin (Syracuse: Syracuse Univ.

Press, 1965), p. 290.

Poem or short story

Bibliography:

Bly, Robert. "The Great Society." In The Light Around the Body.

    New York: Harper & Row, 1967.

Note:

[6] Robert Bly, "The Great Society," in The Light Around the

Body (New York: Harper & Row, 1967), p. 17

Play or short novel

Bibliography:

Feiffer, Jules. The White House Murder Case. In The

    Best Plays of 1969-1970. Ed. Otis L. Guernsey, Jr.

    New York: Dodd, Mead, 1970, pp. 201-16.

Note:

[7] Jules Feiffer, The White House Murder Case, in The Best Plays of 1969-1970, ed. Otis L. Guernsey, Jr. (New York: Dodd, Mead, 1970), pp. 201-16.

Part of a multivolume work

Bibliography:

Gruver, Rebecca Brooks. An American History. 2nd ed. Reading, Mass.: Addison-Wesley, 1976. Vol. II.

Note:

[8] Rebecca Brooks Gruver, An American History, 2nd ed. (Reading, Mass.: Addison-Wesley, 1976), II, 1012-17.

GOVERNMENT PUBLICATION

Bibliography:

U.S. Cong. Senate. Subcommittee on Intergovernmental Relations of the Committee on Government Relations. Government Economy and Spending Reform Act of 1976: Hearings. 94th Cong., 2nd sess. Washington, D.C.: GPO, 1976.

Note:

[9] U.S. Cong., Senate, Subcommittee on Intergovernmental Relations of the Committee on Government Relations, Government Economy and Spending Reform Act of 1976: Hearings. 94th Cong., 2nd sess. (Washington, D.C.: GPO, 1976), p. 120.

ARTICLES IN PERIODICALS

One author

Bibliography:

Wilson, James Q. "Corruption: The Shame of the States."

Public Interest, No. 2 (1966), pp. 28-38.

Note:

[10] James Q. Wilson, "Corruption: The Shame of the States,"

Public Interest, No. 2 (1966), p. 38.

More than one author

Bibliography:

Armstrong, DeWitt C., III, and George A. Graham. "Ethical

Preparation for the Public Service: The 1970s." Bureaucrat,

4, No. 1 (1975), 5-23.

Note:

[11] DeWitt C. Armstrong III and George A. Graham, "Ethical

Preparation for the Public Service: The 1970s," Bureaucrat, 4,

No. 1 (1975), 18.

(Note that p. and pp. are not used to indicate pages when a periodical's volume number is given. The abbreviations are used in all other cases, including when an issue number alone is given. No abbreviation precedes a volume number.)

Anonymous author

Bibliography:

"Lavelle's Private War." Time, 26 June 1972, p. 16.

Note:

[12] "Lavelle's Private War," _Time_, 26 June 1972, p. 16.

Monthly magazine

Bibliography:

Schuck, Peter. "The Curious Case of the Indicted Meat Inspectors."
  Harper's, Sept. 1972, pp. 81-88.

Note:

[13] Peter Schuck, "The Curious Case of the Indicted Meat
Inspectors," _Harper's_, Sept. 1972, p. 86.

Weekly magazine or newspaper

Bibliography:

Griffith, Thomas. "Corruption in the U.S.: Do They All Do It?"
  Time, 31 Dec. 1973, pp. 16-17.

Note:

[14] Thomas Griffith, "Corruption in the U.S.: Do They All
Do It?" _Time_, 31 Dec. 1973, pp. 16-17.

Daily newspaper

Bibliography:

Miller, Harriet. "How Do We Face Our Own 'Abscams'?" _New
  York Times_, Late City Ed., 25 Jan. 1981, Sec. 3, p. 6,
  col. 3.

Note:

[15] Harriet Miller, "How Do We Face Our Own 'Abscams'?"
New York Times, Late City Ed., 25 Jan. 1981, Sec. 3, p. 6,
col. 3.

Journal with pages numbered continuously throughout the year

Bibliography:

Cronin, Thomas E. "A Resurgent Congress and the Imperial
Presidency." Political Science Quarterly, 95 (1980),
209-37.

Note:

[16] Thomas E. Cronin, "A Resurgent Congress and the Imperial
Presidency," Political Science Quarterly, 95 (1980), 224.

Journal with pages separately numbered for each issue

Bibliography:

Schelling, Thomas C. "The Intimate Contest for Self-Command."
Public Interest, No. 60 (1980), pp. 94-118.

Note:

[17] Thomas C. Schelling, "The Intimate Contest for Self-Command,"
Public Interest, No. 60 (1980), p. 103.

OTHER SOURCE MATERIALS

Films

Bibliography:

Pakula, Alan, dir. <u>All the President's Men</u>. With Dustin Hoffman
    and Robert Redford. Warner Brothers. 1975.

Note:

[18] Alan Pakula, dir., <u>All the President's Men</u>, with Dustin
Hoffman and Robert Redford, Warner Brothers, 1975.

Radio or television broadcast

Bibliography:

<u>CBS Evening News with Walter Cronkite</u>. Narr. Walter Cronkite.
    CBS, 20 Oct. 1973.

Note:

[19] <u>CBS Evening News with Walter Cronkite</u>, narr. Walter Cronkite,
CBS, 20 Oct. 1973.

Sound recording

Bibliography:

Frye, David. <u>I Am the President</u>. Elecktra, EKS-75006, n.d.

Note:

[20] David Frye, <u>I Am the President</u>, Elektra, EKS-75006, n.d.

Interview with the source

Bibliography:

Moynihan, Daniel Patrick.   Telephone interview.   25 June 1981.

Note:

[21] Telephone interview with Daniel Patrick Moynihan, United States Senator from New York, 25 June 1981.

Unpublished written material

Bibliography:

Waldo, Dwight.   "Ethical Obligations and Public Service: A Mapping Expedition."   Syracuse Univ.   March 1977.

Note:

[22] Dwight Waldo, "Ethical Obligations and Public Service: A Mapping Expedition," Syracuse Univ.   March 1977.

Picture, graph, chart, or other illustration

Bibliography: No entry needed.

Note: Place the source note directly below the illustration:

Source: James MacGregor Burns, J. W. Peltason, and Thomas E. Cronin, Government by the People, 11th ed. (Englewood Cliffs, N.J.:   Prentice-Hall, 1981), p. 353.

If you have a source that doesn't fit any of the preceding formats, you can find a fuller range of bibliographical and note formats in the *MLA Handbook*.

Determine the Final Format

Often, you will be given a format to use for the final copy of your research paper. If you're not given one, see Step Seven (page 155).

If you are using the endnote style recommended in this book, put the notes at the end of the paper, preceding the bibliography. Two inches down from the top of the page, center the word *Notes*. Then quadruple-space and begin the list of double-spaced notes, indenting the first line of each note five spaces.

For the bibliography, begin with the word *Bibliography* two inches down from the top of the page and centered. Then quadruple-space and begin the bibliography, double-spacing within and between entries, indenting the second and following lines of each entry five spaces.

As you proofread your final copy, be sure that quotations and statistics are accurate. Following are the outline (Step 3), rough draft (Step 4), revised draft (Step 5), and final, refined and recopied, draft (Steps 6 and 7) of a research paper based on the controlling idea "Richard Nixon committed corrupt acts as president that justified his being driven from office." Trace the writer's progress through the last five steps of the process.

Controlling idea: Richard Nixon committed corrupt acts as president

    that justified his being driven from office.

Pattern of development: Narration (and argument)

Order: Chronological (with possible flashbacks)

    I.   Introduction (2-3 paragraphs)

   II.   The Huston plan, 1969

        A. 17 wiretaps on aides and newsmen

        B. Secret police force

            1. Edward Kennedy at Chappaquiddick

            2. John Kennedy and Diem

  III.   The Fielding burglary, 1971

        A. The "Pentagon Papers" and Ellsberg

        B. Hunt and Liddy

   IV.   The "Plumbers"

        A. Blackmailing Edward Kennedy

        B. Firebombing Brookings

    V.   Watergate, June 1972

        A. Strategically senseless

        B. Mitchell's claims of innocence

        C. O'Brien's response

        D. Seven indictments

        E. Convictions

        F. Senate investigation

        G. Nixon and Dean cover-up

        H. McCord letter to Sirica

        I. White House purge

   VI.   Other unethical activities

        A. Colson, Hunt, and ITT scandal

    B. "Dirty tricks"

        1. Rigging polls

        2. phony telegrams

        3. phony ads

        4. Muskie "Canuck" letter

    C. Shumway and Mankiewicz statements

    D. Nixon memoirs explanation

    E. Chile

VII. The continuing investigation

    A. Sequence of events (note cards 20-28)

    B. Allegations against Nixon (note card 9)

    C. Vesco and Rebozo

VIII. Conclusion

ROUGH   DRAFT

Nixon and Watergate ← (improve)

(INTRODUCTION   (2 ¶s?))

However, much earlier --   5/12/69
(Within months of Nixon's inauguration (find date) the first of

seventeen "national security" wiretaps on White House aids and newsmen

was installed.(Final Days, p.510) By July 23, 1970, Nixon has authorized

in writing a plan, "parts of which were clearly illegal" according to

the White House aide who developed it, to improve domestic intelligence

gathering. (Final Days p. 18--apparently rescinded later on)
          in effect
     Nixon created his own police force. Their first job was to investi-

gate Senator Kennedy's accident at Chappaquicick. Later they were

instructed to forge cabels and "create 'evidence'" of John Kennedy's

nonexistent role in the assassinztion of South Vietnamese president

Diem. (Wills, p. 547)   *FLASHBACK — move down*

     According to John Ehrlichman, (find title) the "seminal Watergate
                              1971
episode" was the September 3 and 4 burgarly of the office of Daniel

Ellsberg's psychiatrist, Dr. Lewis Fielding. (Ehrlichman, p. 364)

Ellsberg had "leaked" the "Pentagon Papers" to the New York Times

and the Times had begun to publish them in June 1971. In the name of

national security, White House aides E. Howard Hunt (a former CIA
                                        B
operative) and G. Gordon Liddy (a former FBI agent) supervised the

break-in at Fielding office in the hopes of finding information that

could be used to embarrass Ellsberg. (Hersh, May, p. 63) Ehrlichman

writes, I am now convinced that Nixon perpetrated the Fielding break-in."

(Ehrlichman, p. 369)

     With the "Pentagon Papers" leak, Nixon could charge with some credi-

bility that a conspiracy threatened nationals security. In retaliation for Ellsberg's leak of information that the public deserved to know about,

__Times__ reporter Seymour Hersh reports, "[Nixon] 'told Ehlichman to put

a non-legal team on the conspiracy'--and thes the Plumbers' unit was born."

(Hersh , May, p. 57) "Plumbers" was a new name for new ~~personall~~ personnel in a new

unit doing the same old thing.

The world may never know all the activities in which ~~thtr~~ the Plumbers

engaged between their creation and June 17 1972 when five burglars were

arested in the Democratic headquareto ters at the Watergate Hotel complex.

However, the Plumbers were not idell. One plumbing project called for the

seduction of all the women at the party that Esward Kennedy had attended

on the night of his accicent in order to "backmail them into blackmailing

~~Ed~~ Ted Kennedy." (Wills, p. 548) Anfoher bizare plan was to steal classified

papers from the Brookings IAstitution, the liberal Washington think tank.

Morfin Halperin and Leslie Gelb had left Kissinger's staff and gone to

Brookings, and Nixon believed that they had taken potentially embarrassing

Whfile House documents with them. Hersh reports that Nixon, in a rage,

Complained, "They've got stuff over there . . .stuff that we can't even

get [from~~ oh~~ the Pentagon]. H.R. Haldeman, Nixon's Chief of Staff and most

trusted aide, then took Charles Colson, Special Counfel to the president

(?) and __de facto__ chief of the White House secret police, aside and said

"Well, you heard the President. Take care of Aell." (Hersh, May, p. 56)

The result was the serious discussion of a plan--of which Nixon would

have full knowledge (Ehrlichman, p. 368)--to fire-bomb Brookings: Liddy

and Hunt would buy a used fire engine and fire-fighting uniforms for a

squad Ad Cubans trained to act like firemen; Brookings would be booby

trapped with delayed timing incendiary devices; the Cubans would respond

to the fire alarm and steal the papers. Sources disagree as to why the plan

was not followed through. (Quote Ehrlichman , p. 368, __APM__, p. 355, and Hersh, May, p. 63)

In the light of this kind of activity, Watergate is believable.

~~The Watergate burglary made little sense in June 1972.~~ At the time,

any risk of scandﬁle on Nixon's part seemed highly u̶nlikely; the Demo-

cratic convention was a month ~~way~~ *away* and the party was in disarray; Nixon

leⁱd all theⁱannounced Democratic candidates by no less than nineteen

points. McGoverⁿr, whom Nixon considered the weakest potential opponent

was emerging as the likely nominee. (APM, p. 19) The denial of any

administration involvement by Joʰn Mitchell, former attorⁿᵉy general and

Nixon's campaign manager sounded honest⁚ (note card 17) Mitchell's

Democratic counterpart, Lawrence F. O'Brien, appeared to be *slinging mud* ~~exaggerating~~

when he argued that the break-in (note card 18)

Connections between the five burglars, Hunt and Liddy, and the

Committe to Re-Elect the President (CREP) were quickly established, and

all seven were indicted in September. From the time of their arrests

through their c̶r̶iminal trial in Janua̶r̶t 1973, the seven defendants

maintained their silence, which had been ~~bouth~~. *bought.*

→ INSERT *Haldeman - Helms memo - note cards 10 & 11* ←

The burglars' trial judge, John J. Sirica, suspected a conspiracy

involving impo̶rtant administration officⁱᵃˡˢ. ~~ials.~~ However, five *of* t̶o̶ those

a̶rested entered guilty pelas, and Liddy and James W. M̶cCord refused to

testify in their own behalf and were convicted⁚ *,especially the Wash. Post, the NY Times, and Time,* Had the press, not cont⁻

despite Nixon's opposition, inued to probe the affair and the Senate , not voted 70-0 to conduct its

own investigation, Watergate m̶i̶g̶h̶t̶ *might* have ended with the sentencing of

the burglars.

The Senate investigation led to a renewal of the presedent's active

role in the cover-up, and he began consulting Dean regularʸly about the

contineud silence of the burglars. By March 1973, according to Dean's

Senate testimony, he had frequently discussed the cover-ᵘ̶p with the

president. On March 21, Nixon blocked out the scenario for lying to a

grand jury" and asked Dean how much additional "hush money" the coverup would cost. Dean advised that $1 million would cover the burglars' black-

mail demands, and later in the day, Hunt's lawyer received $75,000. (Final

Days, pp. 107, 28) *The cover-up no longer had much to do with Watergate-- bigger stakes were involved. (APM, p. 349)*

However, the escalating cover-up began to fall apart only two days

afterward when *the* convicted McCord, in an apparent attack of remorse,

wrote to Judge Sirica charging that he and the other defendents were

pressured to plead guilty and reamin *silent,* that perjury was committed

during the trial, and that the break-in involved high-ranking administra-

tion and CREP officials. Five weeks later, on April 30, Nixon *announced The resignations of Haldeman, Ehrlichman, and Atty. Gen'l Kleindienst, and The dismissal of Dean, as well as The appointment of Transp. Sec'y Elliot Richardson to succeed Kleindienst.*

As Nixon was struggling to separate himself from Watergate, Woodward

and Bernstein were uncovering an extraordinary program of campaign abuses.

Their first discovery, later confirmed by the Justice Department (which

despite pressure, was conducting its investigation) (APM, p. 283), grew

out of a Newsday story that Colson had *dispatched* Hunt to Denver in

1972 to visit Dita Beard, *Mrs. Beard, an ITT employee,* had claimed that there was a connection

between ITT's promise of several hundred thousand dollars to the Republi-

lican convention and a favorable anti-trust settledment for ITT.

(APM, pp. 282-83) Woodward and Bernstein were able, *by interviewing Confidential sources,* to confirm that

Colson through Hunt, had contrived to discredit Beard's story and elicit

a statement form her that seh snd the "whole American government" were

"the vicitms of a cruel fraud." She had previously confirmed the

suthenticity of her information to the press. (APM, p. 284)

The Hunt-Colson connection returned the reporters to The Plumbers. This time

Woodward and Bernstein discovered a second echelon of undercover

operatives--a "dirty tricks" squad. The activities that these public

servants and CREP officials performed included rigging polls, sending

phony telegrams to the White House supporting the president's decision to mine Haiphong, ~~planint~~ planting phony "public citizen" ads in newspaſpers,

creating and arranging the publications of a letter--p͟u͟rportedly written

by presidentﾛﾘl candidate Edmund Muskie--th a͟t included the ethnic slur

"Canuck," and generally sabota g ing political opposition. (A͟P͟M͟, pp. 293-94)

A Justice Department official told Bernstein, "Iｆ was basic strategy--

basic strategy that [went] all the way to the top." (A͟P͟M͟, p. 133)

DeVan Shumway, CREP's director af public affaﾛﾘs and a former

White House ｆress aide, admitted these corrupt(if not technically

illegal)activites with shameless candor: "We assumed the other side

would do it also." Frank Mankiewicz of the McGovern campaign responded,

It didn't occur to us. . . These guys are something. They assume we

have the same sleazy tactics as theirs. (A͟P͟M͟, p. 295)

Nixon could not accept the possiblity that his actions were diff-

erent from anyone else's. In his memoirs he continued to justify dirty

tﾛﾘcks: (Note cards 23, 24)

As Ga r y Wills observes, "Ric h ard Nixon, from his need to struggle,

stole the Whi t e House from Richard Nixon. (Wills, p. 550)

The campaign hiﾚﾘﾘinks had an overseas parallel. Seymour Hｅrsh,

in the December 1982 A͟t͟l͟a͟n͟t͟i͟c͟,describes administration efforts during

the fall of 1970 to prevent the election, and ~~tｅﾓﾓ~~ then the inauguration, of

Chilean president Allende. The attempt to block the Cuban-backed, Marx-

ist Allende's election failed: he was elected popularly and then con-

firmed by a natinal legislature that the Nixon adminstration believed

it had securely ~~booﾚﾘﾘy~~ bought, through the CIA, with money provided by three

of Nixon's "corporate benefactors--"Jay Parkinson of Anaconda Copper,

Donald Kendall of Pepsico, and, interestingly, Harold Geneen of ITT.

(Hersh, Dec., p. 58) The result was a second effort: (ntoe card 53)

Hersh quotes Cord Meyer, "one of Richard Helms' most trusted deputies: (Note card 30)
Hersh adds, "Meyer does not say so, but surely there were doubts about the legality of thds President's directive." Hẖrsh goes on:
(note cards 31, 32)

During the spring of 1973 judicial and congressional inquiries into Watergate were accelerating and Nixon was trying to stop them. On May 17 the Senat͠e Watergate Committee under Senator Sam Ervin began its ͜televised hearings. The following day Richardson appointed a special prosectuor, Archibald Cox, and the president delivered a 4,000 word statement in which he denied any knowledge of the burglary and coverup. The events of that summer and fall are history: (<u>Final Days</u>, pp. 510-514) after weeks of uncovering incriminating evidence, Cox subpoenaed Nixon's tapes--secret recordings of all that was discussed in the Oval Office; Nixon refused to yield the tapes and fired Cox, forcing the resignation /ƀơ/ Richardson and D͡puty Attorney General Ruckelshaus; three days later, amid public outerage, 22 bills calling for Nixon's impeachment were introduced in the House, which empowered its Judiciary Committee, under Peter Rodino, to conduct an impeachment investigation; on November 1, Nixon was compelled to name a new special prosecutor; Nixon's lawyers urged his resignation and advise̅d Judge Sirica that some of the subpoened tapes were missing and that other͜s had crucial gaps (<u>Final Days</u> pp. 5-10); Nixon, on November 17, a̅fter being asked on national television abo/ʀ̃ư/ apparent cheating on his 1970 and 1971 income taxes, rambled on about a "1958 oldsmobile in need of an overhaul" and announced,͘ "I am not a crook." (<u>Final Days</u>, p. 89) on March 1, 1974, the grand jury indicted Haldeman, Ehrlichman, and others, and secretly named Nixon an unindicted coconspirator; efforts /ɑ̇ɣ/ obtain further tapes failed, as Nixon claimed executive privilege; the Supreme Court, offended by

Nixon's behavior (<u>Final Days</u> , p. 218), ruled 8-0 that the tapes be

turned over; the House Judiciary Committee passed three articles of im-

peachment, which cited the Watergate burglary and charged the president

with obstructing justice. The president resigned in disgrace on August

9, 1974, after fighting all requests for clarification for more than two years.

On becoming president, Gerald Ford pardoned Richard Nixon for any

illegal acts he might have committed as president. The full pardon was

as controversial as the catalog of allegations against the president

was extensive: (Note card 9))

In additon, two of Nixon's close associates--a swindler (now a

fugitive) named Robert Vesco and the president's best friend, "Bebe"

Rebozo--were under investigation for handling illegal contributions.

(conclusion) ---> Nixon deserved to be
         driven from office

Revised Draft

Watergate and Beyond — (?)

Richard Nixon committed corrupt acts as president that justified his
being driven from office. Nixon will no doubt continue to plead that he
is innocent af all but the most general wrongdoing; he appears to have
(but not his lawyers)
persuaded himself‚ that his role in the Watergate scandal was minimal and
excusable.' (Final Days, pp. 30-41) The Watergate affair was the
most publicized and sensational evidence of Nixon's corruption--it led
to his resignation--but as continuing press investigations reveal, Water-
a symptom   *environment*
gate was only ‚an outward sign of an extremely sinister‚climate of
intrigue, duplicity, and distr/ust in the White House. Watergate was
paranoia?
an example of the Nixon administrationஇ paranoid methods of operation,
domestic and overseas
which included a systematic program to destroy all‚opposition.

"Corruption once wore ªplainer face," wrote Thomas Griffith in
Time a year and a half after the arrest of the Watergate burglars:
INSERT   ⅃
(note card 3) Senator Edward Kennedy was more blunt: "I know the
³
people around Nixon . . . They're thugs. (APM, p. 274) Most were
lawyers as well.
⸢Nixon's thugs were a new breed.
⸢Past administrations--notably Grant's and Harding's--had been
tainted by scandal, but the crimes committed had been the resuℓl) of
ґ   *if?*
simple greed. (Lockard, pp. 477-78.) The public can understand (but
not tolerate) an ABSCAM; also comprehensible is the "vote early and
vote often" school of election rigging. Traditional violators of the
public trust are not even authomatically despised by their constituents:
Boston's popular James Michael Curley was reelected mayor while on his
way to jail for mail fraud; the rogues of Boss Tweed's Tammany Hall
5
remained heroes in some quarters as feeders of the poor.' (Lockard, pp.

477-78) Finding redeeming aspects of Nixon's character, however, is

more difficult. (AGNEW?)

    According to John Ehrlichman, the president's third-in-command and
Assistant to the Pres. for Domestic Affairs
(~~find title~~), the "seminal Watergate episode" was the September 3 and
,1971   Dr. Lewis Fielding,
4 burglary of the office of Daniel Ellsberg's psychiartrist. ~~Dr. Lewis

Fielding.~~ (Ehrlichman, p. 364) Ellsberg, a former Pentagon official

and an associate of Henry Kissinger,'s had "leaked" the "Pentagon

Papers", which detailed the secret bombing of Cambodia, to the New

York Times. ~~and~~ The Times had begun to publish them in June 1971.   In

the name of national security, White House aides E. Howard Hunt (a

former CIA operative) and G. Gordon Liddy (a former FBI agent) super-

vised a break-in at Fielding's office in the hopes of finding information

that could be used to embarrass and discredit Ellsberg.[7] (Hersh, May,

p. 63) Ehrlichman wtites, "I am now convinced that Nixon perpetrated

the Fielding break-in."[8] (Ehrlichman, p. 369)
                    Cloak-and-dagger operations were standard procedure.
What Ehrlichman does not say is that within months of Nixon's

inauguration--on May 12, 1969--the first of seventeen "national

security" wiretaps on White House aides and newsmen was installed

(Final Days, p. 510) Almost a year before the publication of the
                    The Husten
"Pentagon Papers," Nixon had authorized in writing a plan, "parts of
                    Tom Charles Huston,
which were clearly illegal" according to the White House aide who dev-

eloped it, to improved domestic intelligence gathering without the
                                                            10
knowledge or assistance of legitimate law enforcement authorities.

(Final Days p. 18--apparently rescinded later on) Nixon in fact

created his own police force. Their first job was to investigate
                                        The agents
Senator Kennedy's accident at Chappaquiddick. Later ~~they~~ were instructed
                                    Pres.
to forge cables and "create 'evidence'" of John Kennedy's nonexistent
role
~~tole~~ in the assassination of South Vietnamese president Diem.[11] (Wills,

Revised Draft - 3

p. 547)

With the "Pentagon Papers" leak, Nixon could charge with some credi-

bility that a conspiracy threatened national security. However, Nixon's

security--the ability to cover up secrets--was in far greater danger than

the nation's. In retaliation for Ellsberg's leak of information *to which* the

public, ~~deserved to know about~~ *was [probably] entitled (?)*, Times reporter Seymour Hersh reports,

"[Nixon] 'told Ehrlichman to put a non-legal team on the conspiracy'--

and thus the Plumbers' unit was born." (Hersh, May, p. 57) [12] "Plumbers"

was a new name for new personnel in a new unit doing the same old thing

with the zeal of converts. *continuing a tradition(?)*

The world may never know all the activities in which the Plumbers

engaged between their creation and June 17, 1972, when five burglars were

arrested in the Democratic headquarters at the Watergate Hotel complex.

However, the Plumbers were not idle. One plumbing project called for the

seduction of all the women at the party that Edward Kennedy had attended

on the night of his accident in order to "blackmail them into blackmailing

Ted Kennedy."[13] (Wills, p. 548) Another bizarre plan was to steal class-

ified papers from the Brookings Institution, the liberal Washington think

tank. Morton Halperin and Leslie Gelb, *members of* ~~had left~~ Kissinger's staff, *had quit* and

gone to Brookings, and Nixon believed that they had taken potentially

embarrassing White House documents with them. Hersh reports that Nixon,

in a rage, complained, "They've got stuff over there . . . stuff that

we can't even get [from the Pentagon]." H. R. Haldeman, Nixon's Chief

of Staff and most trusted aide, then took Charles Colson, Special Counsel

to the President and de facto chief of the White House secret police, *(?)*

aside and said, "Well, you heard the President. Take care of it."[14]

(Hersh, May, p. 56) The result was the serious discussion of a plan--

of which Nixon would have full knowledge [15](Ehrlichman, p. 368)--to fire-

Revised Draft - 4

bomb Brookings: Liddy and Hunt would buy a used fire engine and fire-
(Explain Cuban-Plumber connection) ←
fighting uniforms for a squad of Cubans ∧ trained to act like firemen.
then
Brookings would ∧ be booby-trapped with delayed-timing incendiary devices;
and
∧ the Cubans would respond to the fire alarm and steal the papers. Ehrlich-
                                                    16
man claims that he killed the plan; (Ehrlichman, p. 368) Carl Bernstein

and Bob Woodward of the <u>Washington Post</u> report that John Dean, the
                                              17
president's counsel, "turned it off"; (<u>APM</u>, p. 355) Liddy writes that
                                          18
it was rejected as too expensive. (quoted by Hersh, May, p. 63). No one

would argue that it was legal.
                  (which also involved Cuban-Americans)
        Against this background, the Watergate burglary ∧ is more believable

than it seemed in June 1972. At the time, any risk of scandal on Nixon's

part seemed highly unlikely: the Democratic convention was a month away

and the party was in disarray; Nixon led all the announced Democratic
                                          George
candidates by no less than nineteen points. ∧ McGovern, whom Nixon con-

sidered the weakest potential opponent, was emerging as the probable
        19 *(APM, p.19)*   *in Watergate*
nominee.   T∦e denial of any administration involvement ∧ by John Mitchell,

former attorney general and Nixon's campaign manager, was plausible:
    INSERT   *20*
(note card 17) Mitchell's Democratic counterpart, Lawrence F. O'Brien,
                                                        INSERT
appeared to be mud-slinging when he argued that the break-in (note card
    21
18).

        Connections between the five burglars, Hunt and Liddy, and the
                            (or CReEP, to cynics)
Committee to Re-Elect the President (CREP) ∧, were quickly established, and
    the   *Conspirators*
a̶l̶l̶ ∧ seven ∧ were indicted in September. From the time of their arrests

through their criminal trial in January 1973, the seven defendants main-

tained their silence, which had been bought ∧ ⟨*how ?*⟩

        On June 23, less than a week after the arrest, Nixon had met with

Haldeman to discuss using the CIA to impede the FBI's investigation of the

break-in. A memo of Haldeman's meeting later in the day with Ehrlichman,

Revised Draft - 5

CIA Director Richard Helms, and Deputy CIA Director Vernon Walters reveals
the tenor of Nixon's strategy: (note card 11) *INSERT* *22*
Nixon was also in a position to bribe Gray: in exchange for Gray's cooperation, the president could nominate him as permanent director of the
FBI.

The burglars' trial judge, John J. Sirica, suspected a conspiracy
involving important administration officials. However,|five of those
arrested entered guilty pleas, and Liddy and James W. McCord refused to
testify in their own behalf and were convicted. Had the press--particu-
larly the Washington Post, the New York Times, and Time--not continued
to probe the affair, and had the Senate, despite strong opposition from
the White House, not voted 70-0 to conduct its own investigation, Watergate might have ended with the sentencing of the burglars.

The Senate investigation led to a renewal of the president's active
role in the cover-up, and he began consulting Dean regularly about the
continued silence of the burglars. By March 1973, according to Dean's
Senate testimony, he had frequently discussed the cover-up with the president. On March 21, Nixon "blocked out the scenario for lying to a grand
jury" and asked Dean how much additional "hush money" the coverup would
cost. Dean advised that $1 million would cover the burglars' blackmail
demands, and later in the day, Hunt's lawyer received $75,000. *23* (Final
Days, pp. 107, 28) The cover-up at this point no longer had much to do
with Watergate itself; its design was to protect the much larger system
of covert operations involving, among others, Nixon, Haldeman, Ehrlichman,
Dean, and Mitchell. *24* (APM, p. 349)

However, the escalating cover-up began to collapse only two days
afterward when the convicted McCord, in an apparent attack of remorse,
wrote to Judge Sirica charging that he and theother defendants were

pressured to plead guilty and remain silent, that perjury was committed
during the trial, and that the break-in involved high-ranking administration and CREP officials. Five weeks later, on April 30, Nixon announced
the resignations of Haldeman, Ehrlichman, and Attorney General Kleindienst, the dismissal of John Dean, and the appointment of Transportation
Secretary Elliot Richardson as Kleindienst's successor.

As Nixon was struggling to insulate himself from Watergate, Woodward
and Bernstein were uncovering an extraordinary program of campaign abuses.
Their first discovery, later confirmed by the Justice Department (which,
despite pressure, was conducting its investigation), (APM, p. 283) grew [25]
out of a Newsday story that Colson had dispatched Hunt to Denver in 1972
to visit Dita Beard. Mrs. Beard, an *International Telephone and Telegraph* (ITT) employee, had claimed that
there was a connection between ITT's promise of several hundred thousand
dollars to the Republican convention and a favorable anti-trust settlement for ITT. (APM, pp. 282-83) Woodward and Bernstein were able, [26]
interviewing confidential sources, to *establish* that Colson, through Hunt,
had contrived to discredit Beard's story and elicit a statement from her
that she and "the whole American government" were the "victims of a
cruel fraud." She had previously confirmed the authenticity of her
information to the press. (APM, p. 284) [27]

The Hunt-Colson connection reopened the reporters' investigation
of the Plumbers. This time they discovered a second echelon of undercover operatives--a "dirty tricks" squad responsible for tampering with
public opinion hostile to the White House. The activities that these
public servants and CREP officials performed included rigging polls,
sending phony telegrams to the White House supporting the president's
unpopular decision to mine Haiphong, planting phony "public citizen" ads in
newspapers, creating and arranging the publication of a letter--pur-

Revised Draft - 7

portedly written by presidential candidate Edmund Muskie--expressing con-

tempt for Americans of French-Canadian ancestry, and generally sabotaging

political opposition. (APM, pp. 293-94) A Justice Department official [28]

told Bernstein, "It was strategy--basic strategy that [went] all the way

to the top." (APM, p. 133) [29]

DeVan L. Shumway, CREP's director of public affairs and a former

White House press aide, admitted these corrupt (if not technically illegal)

activities with shameless candor: "We assumed the other side would do it

also." Frank Mankiewicz of the McGovern campaign responded, "It didn't

occur to us . . . These guys are something. They assume we have the same

sleazy tactics as theirs." (APM, p. 295) [30]

Nixon could not accept the possibility that his actions were diff-
(Add Schultz, Walters, and IRS - McGovern contributor) [31]
erent from anyone else's. In his memoirs, he continued to justify dirty

tricks: (Note cards 23, 24) INSERT [32]

No ?
As Gary Wills observes, "Richard Nixon, from his need to struggle,

stole the White House from Richard Nixon." (Wills, p. 550) [33]

The campaign highjinks were nothing compared with what the admin-

istration was doing abroad. Seymour Hersh, in the December 1982 Atlantic,

describes administration efforts during the fall of 1970 to prevent the

election, and then the inauguration of Chilean president Allende. [34] The

attempt to block the Cuban-backed, Marxist Allende's election failed: he

was elected popularly and then confirmed by a national legislature that

the Nixon administration believed it had securely bought, through the CIA,

with money provided by three of Nixon's "corporate benefactors"--Jay

Parkinson of Anaconda Copper, Donald Kendall of Pepsico, and, interest-

ingly, Harold Geneen of ITT. [35] (Hersh, Dec., p. 58) The result was a

second effort: (note card 53) INSERT [36]

Hersh quotes Cord Meyer, "one of Richard Helms's most trusted

Revised Draft - 8

INSERT
deputies: (note card 30)

Hersh adds, "Meyer does not say so, but surely there were doubts about
the legality of the President's directive."[37] Hersh goes on: (note cards *INSERT*
31, 32)[38]

During the spring of 1973 judicial and congressional inquiries into
Watergate were accelerating and Nixon was trying to stop them. On May
17 the Senate Watergate Committee under Senator Sam Ervin began its
televised hearings. The following day Richardson appointed a special
prosecutor, Archibald Cox, and the president delivered a 4,000-word statement in which he denied any knowledge of the burglary and cover-up. The
events of that summer and fall are history: (*Final Days*, pp. 510-514)[39]
after weeks of uncovering incriminating evidence, Cox subpoenaed Nixon's
famous
tapes--secret recordings of all that was discussed in the Oval Office;
Nixon refused to yield the tapes and fired Cox, forcing the resignations
of Richardson and Deputy Attorney General Ruckelshaus; three days later,
amid public outrage, 22 bills calling for Nixon's impeachment were
introduced in the House, which empowered its Judiciary Committee, under
Peter Rodino, to conduct an impeachment investigation. On November 1,
Nixon was compelled to name a new special prosecutor; Nixon's lawyers
urged his resignation and advised Judge sirica that some of the subpoenaed tapes were missing and that others had crucial gaps. (*Final Days*,[40]
pp. 5-10). Nixon, on November 17, after being asked on national television
about apparent cheating on his 1970 and 1971 income taxes, rambled about
a "1958 Oldsmobile in need of an overhaul" and announced, "I am not a
crook" (*Final Days*, p. 83).[41] On March 1, 1974, the grand jury indicted
Haldeman, Ehrlichman, and others, and secretly named Nixon an unindicted
coconspirator. Efforts to obtain further tapes failed, as Nixon claimed
and
executive privilege; the Supreme Court, offended by Nixon's behavior,[42]

(Final Days, p. 218) / ruled 8-0 that the tapes be turned over. The House

Judiciary Committee passed three articles of impeachment, which cited the

Watergate burglary and charged the president with obstructing justice.

The president resigned in disgrace on August 9, 1974, after fighting all

requests for clarification, *of Watergate* for more than two years.

On becoming the thirty-eighth president of the United States, Gerald

Ford pardoned Richard Nixon for any illegal acts he might have committed

as president. The full pardon was as controversial as the catalog of

allegations against the president was extensive: (note card 9) *INSERT* 43

In addition, two of Nixon's close associates--*an accused* swindler (now a

fugitive) named Robert Vesco and the president's best friend, "Bebe"

Rebozo--were under investigation for handling illegal *Campaign* contributions.

All of these allegations, as well as ~~his~~ *Nixon's* maintenance of a secret police

force, and what is now know about his involvement *that regularly broke the law* in even more reprehensible

plotting overseas, (deserve) explanations. The picture they paint is hardly

"presidential." Nixon probably ~~deserved~~ *merited* harsher treatment than being

driven from office. Nonetheless, he prolonged his own suffering through

his vain and obstinate refusal to leave office gracefully, and some will

argue that he paid his dues to the millions he misled and the office that

he violated.

Research Paper, refined and recopied (final draft)

Cary Rand

Professor Frederick

Government 101

May 20, 1983

The Corruption of the President, 1969-1974

Richard Nixon committed corrupt acts as president that justified his being driven from office. Nixon will no doubt continue to plead that he is innocent of all but the most general wrongdoing; he appears to have persuaded himself (if not his lawyers and the public) that his role in the Watergate scandal was minimal and excusable.[1] The Watergate affair was the most publicized and sensational evidence of Nixon's corruption--it led to his resignation. As continuing press investigations reveal, however, Watergate was only a symptom of an extremely sinister environment of intrigue, duplicity, and distrust in the Nixon White House. Watergate was an example of the Nixon administration's paranoiac methods of operation--the visible tip of an iceberg-- which included a systematic program to destroy all opposition, domestic as well as international.

"Corruption once wore a plainer face," wrote Thomas Griffith in Time a year and a half after the arrest of the Watergate burglars: "The transgressions of Watergate and the Nixon palace guard turn more on amorality than immorality and are all the more pernicious for that. These were power-intoxicated, self-righteous men."[2] Senator Edward Kennedy was more blunt: "I know the people around Nixon. . . . They're thugs."[3] Most were lawyers as well.

The associates whom Richard Nixon chose to run the country with him were a new breed of thug. Past administrations--notably Grant's

final draft--2

and Harding's--had been tainted by scandal, but the crimes committed had been the result of simple greed.[4] The public can understand (if not tolerate) an ABSCAM; also comprehensible is the "vote early and vote often" school of election rigging. Traditional violators of the public trust are not even automatically despised by their constituents: Boston's popular James Michael Curley was reelected mayor while on his way to jail for mail fraud; the rogues of Boss Tweed's Tammany Hall remained heroes in some quarters as feeders of the poor.[5] Even Spiro Agnew is remembered more as Nixon's court jester than as a crooked governor of Maryland. Finding likable aspects of Nixon's character, however, is difficult.

According to John Ehrlichman, the president's third-in-command and Assistant to the President for Domestic Affairs, the "seminal Watergate episode" was the September 3 and 4, 1971, burglary of the office of Dr. Lewis Fielding, Daniel Ellsberg's psychiatrist.[6] Ellsberg, a former Pentagon official and an associate of Henry Kissinger, had "leaked" the "Pentagon Papers," which detailed the secret bombing of Cambodia, to the New York Times. The Times had begun to publish them in June 1971. In the name of national security, White House aides E. Howard Hunt (a former CIA operative) and G. Gordon Liddy (a former FBI agent) supervised a break-in at Fielding's office in the hopes of finding information that could be used to embarrass and discredit Ellsberg.[7] Ehrlichman writes, "I am now convinced that Nixon perpetrated the Fielding break-in."[8]

What Ehrlichman does not say is that cloak-and-dagger operations were already standard procedure at the Nixon White House. Within months of Nixon's inauguration--on May 12, 1969--the first of seventeen "national security" wiretaps on White House aides and newsmen was installed.[9] Almost a year before the publication of the "Pentagon Papers," Nixon had authorized in writing the Huston plan, "parts of which were clearly

final draft--3

illegal" according to Tom Charles Huston, the White House aide who developed it, to improve domestic intelligence gathering without the knowledge or assistance of legitimate law enforcement authorities.[10] Nixon in fact created his own police force, whose first job was to investigate Senator Kennedy's accident at Chappaquiddick. Later these undercover agents were instructed to forge cables and "create 'evidence'" of President John Kennedy's nonexistent role in the assassination of South Vietnamese president Diem.[11]

With the "Pentagon Papers" leak, Nixon could charge with some credibility that a conspiracy threatened national security. However, Nixon's security--the ability to cover up secrets--was in far greater danger than the nation's. In retaliation for Ellsberg's leak of information to which the public was probably entitled, Times reporter Seymour Hersh reports, "[Nixon] 'told Ehrlichman to put a non-legal team on the conspiracy'--and thus the Plumbers' unit was born."[12] "Plumbers" was a new name for new personnel in a new unit continuing a tradition of espionage with the zeal of converts.

The world may never know all the activities in which the Plumbers engaged between their creation and June 17, 1972, when five burglars were arrested in the Democratic headquarters at the Watergate Hotel complex. However, the Plumbers were not idle. One plumbing project called for the seduction of all the women at the party that Edward Kennedy had attended on the night of his accident in order to "blackmail them into blackmailing Ted Kennedy."[13] Another bizarre plan was to steal classified papers from the Brookings Institution, the liberal Washington think tank.

Morton Halperin and Leslie Gelb, members of Kissinger's staff, had quit and gone to Brookings, and Nixon believed that they had taken

final draft--4

potentially embarrassing White House documents with them. Hersh reports

that Nixon, in a rage, complained, "They've got stuff over there . . .

stuff that we can't even get [from the Pentagon]." H. R. Haldeman,

Nixon's Chief of Staff and most trusted aide, then took Charles Colson,

Special Counsel to the President and de facto chief of the White House

secret police, aside and said, "Well, you heard the President. Take

care of it."[14] The result was serious discussion of a plan--of which

Nixon would have full knowledge[15]--to fire-bomb Brookings: Liddy and

Hunt would buy a used fire engine and fire-fighting uniforms for a squad

of Cubans (the Plumbers relied on the anti-communist sympathies of

expatriot Cubans) trained to act like firemen. Brookings would then be

booby-trapped with delayed-timing incendiary devices, and the Cubans

would respond to the fire alarm and steal the papers. Ehrlichman claims

that he killed the plan;[16] Carl Bernstein and Bob Woodward of the

Washington Post report that John Dean, the president's counsel, "turned

it off";[17] Liddy writes that it was rejected as too expensive.[18] No one

would argue that it was legal.

Against this background, the Watergate burglary (which also involved

Cuban-Americans) is more believable than it seemed in June 1972. At the

time, any risk of scandal on Nixon's part seemed highly unlikely: the

Democratic convention was a month away and the party was in disarray;

Nixon led all the announced Democratic candidates by no less than nine-

teen points. George McGovern, whom Nixon considered the weakest potential

opponent, was emerging as the probable nominee.[19] The denial by John

Mitchell, former attorney general and Nixon's campaign manager, of any

administration involvement in the Watergate affair was plausible: "There

is no place in this campaign or in the electoral process for this type

of activity, and we will not permit or condone it."[20] Mitchell's

final draft--5

Democratic counterpart, Lawrence F. O'Brien, appeared to be mud-slinging

when he argued that the break-in "raised the ugliest questions about the

integrity of the political process. . . . No mere statement of innocence

by Mr. Nixon's campaign manager . . . will dispell these questions. " 21

Connections between the five burglars, Hunt and Liddy, and the

Committee to Re-Elect the President (CREP, irreverently referred to as

CReEP) were quickly established, and the seven conspirators were indicted

in September. From the time of their arrests through their criminal trial

in January 1973, the defendants maintained their silence, which had been

bought with cash, intimations of executive clemency, and assurances that

the government's investigation would be less than thorough.

On June 23, less than a week after the arrests, Nixon had met with

Haldeman to discuss using the CIA to impede the FBI's investigation of

the break-in. A memo of Haldeman's meeting later in the day with Ehrlich-

man, CIA Director Richard Helms, and Deputy CIA Director Vernon Walters

reveals the tenor of Nixon's strategy:

> . . . it was the President's wish that Walters call on FBI
>
> Acting Director L. Patrick Gray and suggest to him that
>
> since the five suspects had been arrested, this should be
>
> sufficient and that it was not advantageous to have the
>
> inquiry pushed--especially in Mexico, etc. [where the
>
> burglars' "hush money" was laundered by CREP].22

Nixon was also in a position to bribe Gray: in exchange for Gray's

cooperation, the president could nominate him as permanent director of

the FBI.

The burglars' trial judge, John J. Sirica, suspected a conspiracy

involving important administration officials. However, five of those

arrested entered guilty pleas, and Liddy and James W. McCord refused to
testify in their own behalf and were convicted. Had the press--particu-
larly the Washington Post, the New York Times, and Time--not continued to
probe the affair, and had the Senate, despite strong opposition from the
White House, not voted 70-0 to conduct its own investigation, Watergate
might have ended with the sentencing of the burglars.

The Senate investigation led to a renewal of the president's active
role in the cover-up, and he began consulting Dean regularly about the
continued silence of the burglars. By March 1973, according to Dean's
Senate testimony, he had frequently discussed the cover-up with the
president. On March 21, Nixon "blocked out the scenario for lying to a
grand jury" and asked Dean how much additional "hush money" the cover-up
would cost. Dean advised that $1 million would cover the burglars' black-
mail demands, and later in the day, Hunt's lawyer received $75,000.[23]
The cover-up at this point no longer had much to do with Watergate itself;
its design was to protect the much larger system of covert operations
involving, among others, Nixon, Haldeman, Ehrlichman, Dean, and Mitchell.[24]

However, the escalating cover-up began to collapse only two days
afterward when the convicted McCord, in an apparent attack of remorse,
wrote to Judge Sirica charging that he and the other defendants were
pressured to plead guilty and remain silent, that perjury was committed
during the trial, and that the break-in involved high-ranking administration and CREP officials. Five weeks later, on April 30, Nixon announced
the resignations of Haldeman, Ehrlichman, and Attorney General Kleindienst,
the dismissal of John Dean, and the appointment of Transportation Secretary Elliot Richardson as Kleindienst's successor.

As Nixon was struggling to insulate himself from Watergate, Woodward
and Bernstein were uncovering an extraordinary program of campaign abuses.

final draft--7

Their first discovery, later confirmed by the Justice Department (which,

despite pressure, was conducting its investigation),[25] grew out of a

Newsday story that Colson had dispatched to Hunt in Denver in 1972 to visit

Dita Beard. Mrs. Beard, an International Telephone and Telegraph (ITT)

employee, had claimed that there was a connection between ITT's promise of

several hundred thousand dollars to the Republican convention and a fa-

vorable anti-trust settlement for ITT.[26] Woodward and Bernstein were able,

interviewing confidential sources, to establish that Colson, through Hunt,

had contrived to discredit Beard's story and elicit a statement from her

that she and "the whole American government" were "the victims of a cruel

fraud." She had previously confirmed the authenticity of her information

to the press.[27]

The Hunt-Colson connection reopened the reporters' investigation of

the Plumbers. This time they discovered a second echelon of undercover

operatives--a "dirty tricks" squad responsible for tampering with public

opinion hostile to the White House. The activities that these public

servants and CREP officials performed included rigging polls, barraging

the White House with phony telegrams of support to generate favorable

publicity, planting phony "public citizen" ads in newspapers, creating

and arranging the publication of a letter--purportedly written by pres-

idential candidate Edmund Muskie--expressing contempt for Americans of

French-Canadian ancestry, and generally sabotaging political opposition.[28]

A Justice Department official told Bernstein, "It was strategy--basic

strategy that [went] all the way to the top."[29]

DeVan L. Shumway, CREP's director of public affairs and a former

White House press aide, admitted these corrupt (if not technically illegal)

activities with shameless candor: "We assumed the other side would do it

also." Frank Mankiewicz of the McGovern campaign responded, "It didn't

final draft--8

occur to us . . . These guys are something. They assume we have the same

sleazy tactics as theirs."[30] (It later emerged that Nixon, during his

last days as president, was willing to fire George Schultz, his Treasury

Secretary and now Secretary of State, and IRS Commissioner Johnnie Walters

for not cooperating in an effort to uncover damaging information about one

of McGovern's contributors.)[31]

Nixon could not accept the possibility that his actions were extra-

ordinary and, in his memoirs, he continued to justify dirty tricks:

> We were faced in 1960 by an organization that had equal
>
> dedication to ours and unlimited money, that was led by
>
> the most ruthless group of political operators ever
>
> mobilized for a presidential campaign. Kennedy's organi-
>
> zation approached dirty tricks with a roguish relish and
>
> carried them off with . . . insouciance. . . . From this
>
> point on I had the wisdom and wariness of someone who had
>
> been burned by the power of the Kennedys and their money
>
> and by the license they were given by the media. I vowed
>
> that I would never again enter an election at a disadvan-
>
> tage by being vulnerable to them--or anyone--on the level
>
> of political tactics.[32]

As Garry Wills observes, "Richard Nixon, from his need to struggle,

stole the White House from Richard Nixon."[33]

The campaign highjinks were nothing compared with what the admin-

istration was doing abroad. Seymour Hersh, in the December 1982 _Atlantic_,

describes administration efforts during the fall of 1970 to prevent the

election, and then the inauguration, of Chilean president Allende.[34]

The attempt to block the Cuban-backed, Marxist Allende's election

final draft--9

failed: he was elected popularly and then confirmed by a national legis-

lature that the Nixon administration believed it had securely bought,

through the CIA, with money provided by three of Nixon's "corporate

benefactors"--Jay Parkinson of Anaconda Copper, Donald Kendall of Pepsico,

and, interestingly, Harold Geneen of ITT.[35] The result was a second

effort:

> More than $3.5 million was authorized by Nixon and Kissinger
>
> for CIA activities in 1971; by September of 1973, when
>
> Allende was assassinated--or committed suicide--during
>
> a successful military coup, the CIA had spent $8 million,
>
> or at least officially reported spending that much, on
>
> anti-Allende plotting."[36]

Hersh quotes Cord Meyer, "one of Richard Helms's most trusted

deputies":

> . . . We were surprised by what we were being asked to
>
> do . . . The pride we might have felt at having been
>
> among the select few chosen by the President to execute
>
> a secret and important mission was more than counter-
>
> balanced by our doubts about the wisdom of this course.

Hersh adds, "Meyer does not say so, but surely there were doubts about

the legality of the President's directive."[37] Hersh goes on about

Chile:

> . . . official lying and distortion about Chile reached a
>
> point equaled by only one other issue in the Nixon era:
>
> the Watergate break-in with its subsequent cover-up. . . .

final draft--10

> Cover-up payments were sought for CIA contacts and associates
> caught in the act of crime . . . records were destroyed
> and documents distorted . . . [and] much of the official
> testimony . . . was perjury. . . . The White House was
> in league with unscrupulous and violent men who did not
> understand the difference between right and wrong . . .
>
> If Nixon and Kissinger wanted it to be done, it was
> to be done.[38]

During the spring of 1973 judicial and congressional inquiries into
Watergate were accelerating and Nixon was trying to stop them. On May
17 the Senate Watergate Committee under Senator Sam Ervin began its
televised hearings. The following day Richardson appointed a special
prosecutor, Archibald Cox, and the president delivered a 4,000-word
statement in which he denied any knowledge of the burglary and cover-
up. The events of that summer and fall are history:[39] after weeks
of uncovering incriminating evidence, Cox subpoenaed Nixon's notorious
tapes--secret recordings of all that was discussed in the Oval Office;
Nixon refused to yield the tapes and fired Cox, forcing the resignations
of Richardson and Deputy Attorney General Ruckelshaus; three days later,
amid public outrage, twenty-two bills calling for Nixon's impeachment
were introduced in the House, which empowered its Judiciary Committee,
under Peter Rodino, to conduct an impeachment investigation. On November
1, Nixon was compelled to name a new special prosecutor; Nixon's lawyers
urged his resignation and advised Judge Sirica that some of the subpoenaed
tapes were missing and that others had crucial gaps.[40] Nixon, on November
17, after being asked on national television about apparent cheating on
his 1970 and 1971 income taxes, rambled on about a "1958 Oldsmobile in

final draft--11

need of an overhaul" and announced, "I am not a crook."[41] On March 1,

1974, the grand jury indicted Haldeman, Ehrlichman, and others, and

secretly named Nixon an unindicted co-conspirator. Efforts to obtain

further tapes failed, as Nixon claimed executive privilege, and the Supreme

Court, offended by Nixon's behavior,[42] ruled 8-0 that the tapes be turned

over. The House Judiciary Committee passed three articles of impeachment,

which cited the Watergate burglary and charged the president with obstruc-

ting justice. The president resigned in disgrace on August 9, 1974, after

fighting all requests for clarification of Watergate for more than two

years.

On becoming the thirty-eighth president of the United States, Gerald

Ford pardoned Richard Nixon for any illegal acts he might have committed

as president. The full pardon was as controversial as the catalog of

allegations against the president was extensive:

> . . . that International Telephone and Telegraph had
>
> virtually bribed him with a donation to his 1972 re-
>
> election campaign; that he had cheated on his income
>
> taxes; that he had used government funds to vastly
>
> improve his estates in Key Biscayne and at San Clemente;
>
> that he had backdated the deed to his vice-presidential
>
> papers to claim a half-million dollar tax deduction;
>
> . . . that [he] had raised the price of milk supports
>
> in exchange for campaign contributions from the dairy
>
> industry.[43]

In addition, two of Nixon's close associates--an accused swindler

(now a fugitive) named Robert Vesco and the president's best friend,

"Bebe" Rebozo--were under investigation for handling illegal campaign contributions. All of these allegations, as well as Nixon's maintenance

of a secret police force that regularly broke the law, and what is now

known about his involvement in even more reprehensible plotting overseas,

deserve explanations. The picture they paint is hardly "presidential."

Nixon probably merited harsher treatment than being driven from office.

Nonetheless, he prolonged his own suffering through his vain and obstinate

refusal to leave office gracefully, and some will argue that he paid his

dues to the millions he misled and the office that he violated.

Notes

[1] Bob Woodward and Carl Bernstein, The Final Days (New York: Avon, 1977), pp. 30-41.

[2] Thomas Griffith, "Corruption in the U.S.: Do They All Do It?" Time, 31 Dec. 1973, p. 16.

[3] Carl Bernstein and Bob Woodward, All the President's Men (New York: Warner Books, 1975), p. 274.

[4] Duane Lockard, "The 'Great Tradition' of American Corruption," New Society, 31 May 1973, pp. 486-88.

[5] Lockard, p. 487.

[6] John Ehrlichman, Witness to Power: The Nixon Years (New York: Pocket Books, 1982), p. 364.

[7] Seymour M. Hersh, "Kissinger and Nixon in the White House," The Atlantic, 249, No. 5 (May 1982), 63.

[8] Ehrlichman, p. 369.

[9] Woodward and Bernstein, p. 510.

[10] Woodward and Bernstein, p. 18. The authorization was apparently rescinded five days later.

[11] Garry Wills, Nixon Agonistes: The Crisis of the Self-Made Man, rev. ed. (New York: NAL, 1979), p. 547.

[12] Hersh, p. 57.

[13] Wills, p. 548.

[14] Hersh, p. 56.

[15] Ehrlichman, p. 368.

[16] Ehrlichman, p. 368.

[17] Bernstein and Woodward, p. 355.

[18] Hersh, p. 63.

[19] Bernstein and Woodward, p. 19.

[20] Bernstein and Woodward, p. 21.

[21] Bernstein and Woodward, p. 21.

[22] Woodward and Bernstein, p. 19.

[23] Woodward and Bernstein, pp. 28, 107.

[24] Bernstein and Woodward, p. 349.

[25] Bernstein and Woodward, p. 283.

[26] Bernstein and Woodward, p. 283.

[27] Bernstein and Woodward, p. 284.

[28] Bernstein and Woodward, pp. 293-94.

[29] Bernstein and Woodward, p. 133.

[30] Bernstein and Woodward, p. 295.

[31] Woodward and Bernstein, p. 84.

[32] Wills, p. 550.

[33] Wills, p. 550.

[34] Seymour M. Hersh, "The Price of Power: Kissinger, Nixon, and Chile," The Atlantic, 250, No. 6 (Dec. 1982), pp. 31-58.

[35] Hersh, "The Price of Power," p. 58.

[36] Hersh, "The Price of Power," p. 58.

[37] Hersh, "The Price of Power," p. 44.

[38] Hersh, "The Price of Power," p. 45.

[39] Woodward and Bernstein, pp. 510-14, provide a brief chronology of Nixon's presidency.

[40] Woodward and Bernstein, p. 89.

[41] Woodward and Bernstein, pp. 5-10.

[42] Woodward and Bernstein, p. 218.

[43] Woodward and Bernstein, p. 6.

Bibliography

Bernstein, Carl, and Bob Woodward. All the President's Men. New York:

    Warner Books, 1975.

Ehrlichman, John. Witness to Power: The Nixon Years. New York:

    Pocket Books, 1982.

Griffith, Thomas. "Corruption in the U.S.: Do They All Do It?" Time,

    31 Dec. 1973, pp. 16-17.

Hersh, Seymour M. "Kissinger and Nixon in the White House." The

    Atlantic, 249, No. 5 (May 1982), pp. 35-68.

----------. "The Price of Power: Kissinger, Nixon, and Chile." The

    Atlantic, 250, No. 6 (Dec. 1982), pp. 31-58.

Wills, Garry. Nixon Agonistes: The Crisis of the Self-Made Man. Rev.

    ed. New York: NAL, 1979.

Woodward, Bob, and Carl Bernstein. The Final Days. New York: Avon,

    1977.

Index

Abbreviations, 114
Absolute statements, avoiding, 82
Abstract words, 109–110
Active voice, 123–126
Adjectives, vague, 110–111
Adverbs, vague, 110–111
Almanacs, 145
Analogy, 40–42, 50
  defects in, 84
Analysis, 35
  defects in, 84
  paragraph using, 89
Anticlimactic order, 54
Argument, 47–51
  circular, 50
  defects in, 85
Audience analysis, 11–13

Bibliography, 150, 156–165
  format for, 157–165

Bibliography card, 151
Body of written piece, 53
Books
  bibliography entries for, 157–159
  footnote entries for, 157–159
  as sources, 145, 146
Brainstorming, 19–22
  for research paper, 143

Capitalization, 135
Card catalog, 146
Cause
  necessary, 45
  sufficient, 45
  ultimate, 45
Cause and effect, 45–47
  defects in reasoning, 85
Chronological order, 54–55
Circular argument, 50
Classification, 36–38

defects in, 84
Clichés, avoiding, 115
Climactic order, 53–54, 56, 57, 90
Coinages, avoiding, 113–114
Comma splice, 133
Comparison, 38–40, 151
    block method, 39–40
    defects in, 84
    paragraph using, 90
    point-by-point method, 39, 40, 57
Complex sentence, 128, 129
Compound-complex sentence, 133
Compound sentence, 128
Conclusion, 53, 96
Concrete words, 109–110
Connective words and expressions, 91
Connotations, 108
Contrast, 38–40, 151
    block method, 39–40
    defects in, 84
    paragraph using, 90
    point-by-point method, 39, 40
Controlling idea (thesis), 49
    ending with restatement of, 96
    narrowing of, 81
    relevance of content to, 80–81
    of research paper, 143, 151
    statement of, 15, 95
    topic choice and, 14–16
Corrections, 72. *See also* Recopying;
    Refining; Revising
Critics (criticism), 75

Dangling modifier, 134–135
Definition, 42–43
    defects in, 85
Demonstrative pronouns, 93
Denotation, 109
Description, 33
    defects in, 84
Development, patterns of. *See* Pat-
    terns of development
Dictionaries, 144
Draft, writing a, 69–74
    environment and, 70
    equipment for, 69–70

letting loose, 71–73
    preparation for, 70–71
    recopying, 137–140
    refining, 99–136
    of research paper, 152–155
    revising, 77–98
    taking a break after, 74

Editorial symbols, 100
Ellipsis, 156–157
Ellipsis points, 153
Emotional appeal, 50
Emotional associations of words, 108
Encyclopedias, 144
Ending, effective, 96
Entertainment, as purpose in writ-
    ing, 14
Environment, 70
Equipment, 69–70
Evidence, 47–49
Example(s), 43–44, 81
    defects in, 84
    paragraph using, 89
Experience, writing from, 18
Experts, 26–28
Explanation
    process, 34–35
    as purpose in writing, 14

Facts
    accuracy of, 81–82
    opinions as distinct from, 82
    use of specific, 81–82
Fallacies, 49–50
Familiarity with topic, 9
Five *W*'s and *H*, 20–22
Flashback, 55
Footnotes, 73, 155–165
    format for, 156–165
Format, 52–53, 138
    for research paper, 166
Freewriting, 67–74. *See also* Draft
Goals, setting, 70–71
Grammar, 132–136

Humanities Index, 146

Illustration. *See* Example(s)
Information, gathering, 17–29
    brainstorming, 19–22
    from experience, 18
    from experts, 26–28
    from observation, 18–19
    from other sources, 28
    from reading, 22–26
    for research paper, 143–150
Instruction, process, 34–35
Interest in topic, 8
Interviewing, 26–27
    by mail, 27
    in person, 26–27
    by telephone, 26–27
Introduction, 53
    opening paragraph, 94–95
Introductory phrases, unnecessary,
    121–123

Jargon, avoiding, 113

Length of assignment, topic
    choice and, 9–10
Letter, interviewing by, 27
Library, use of, 142–148
Listing, 91

Magazines. *See* Periodicals
Margins, 138
MLA Handbook, 157

Narration, 32
    defects in, 84
Neatness, 137
Newspapers. *See* Periodicals
New York Times Index, 145, 147
Notes
    for research paper, 148–152
    reviewing, 73

Obscurity, 102
Observation, 18–19
Opening paragraph, 94–95
Opinions, facts as distinct from, 82
Order, 51–59
    anticlimactic, 54
    chronological, 54–55
    climactic, 53–54, 57, 58, 91
    coordination of pattern of develop-
        ment and, 56–59
    format, 52–53
    paragraphs and, 91–92
    revising, 85–86
    spatial, 55–58
Organization, 30–66
    coordination of plan, 56–58
    order, 51–59
    patterns of development, 31–49
    of research paper, 150–152
    revising, 85–88
Outline, 59–66
    following order of, 83–84
    formal, 63–66
        sentence outline, 64–65
        topic outline, 64
    inclusion in rewrite of all ideas in, 80
    informal, 59–63
    reviewing, 73

Paragraphs, 85–94
    coherency of, 89–94
    division of, 93
    length of, 93
    order of, 91
    patterns of, 89–90
    transitional, 92
    transitional words and, 92–94
    unified, 86, 87–88
    well-developed, 88–89
Parallel sentence, 130–131
Paraphrasing, 149, 154, 155
Passive voice, 125–126
Patterns of development, 31–49
    analogy, 40–42
    analysis, 35–36
    argument, 47–51

cause and effect, 45–47
classification, 36–37
comparison, 38–40, 151
contrast, 38–40, 151
coordination of order and, 56–59
defects in, 84–85
definition, 42–43
description, 33
example, 43–44
narration, 32
paragraph and, 89–90
process explanation, 34–36
process instruction, 34–36
revising, 84–86
Periodical indexes, 146–147
Periodicals
  bibliography entries for articles in,
    161–163
  footnote entries for articles in,
    161–163
  as sources, 145–147
Periodic sentence, 129
Persuasion, 14
Plagiarism, 23, 154
Point of view, shifts in, 118–119, 130
Preparation for writing, 70–71
Prepositional phrases, shortening
    wordy, 122–123
Pretentiousness, 102
Prewriting, 5–66
  gathering information, 17–29
  organization, 30–66
  topic choice, 7–16
Primary sources, 144–145
Process, 84
Process explanation, 34–36
Process instruction, 34–36
Pronoun reference, 116–117
Pronouns
  demonstrative, 92
  sexist use of, 104–105
  as transitional words, 91–92
Proofreading, 138–139, 166
Punctuation, 132, 135
Purpose
  choice of topic and, 13–15
  statement of, 14–16

Question and answer, paragraph based
  on, 90
Questionnaires, 27
Quotation marks, 23, 153
Quotations, 23, 73
  accuracy of, 81–82
  in research paper, 149, 152–154

Radio, as information source, 28
Reader, topic choice and, 11–13
Reader's Guide to Periodical Literature, 145, 146
Reading, gathering information by,
  22–26
Recopying, 137–144
  format, following a, 138
  neatness in, 137
  proofreading, 138–139
  research paper, 155–165
Reference books, 145
Refining, 99–136
  checklist, use of, 101
  marking the draft, 100
  mechanics, 132–136
  research paper, 155
  sentences, 115–132
  style, 100–106
  word usage, 107–115
Relaxation, 71
Repetition, needless, 120–121
Research paper, 141–166
  bibliography, 156–165
  draft of, 152–155
  determining kinds of sources,
    144–145
  finding sources, 145–147
  footnotes, 156–165
  library, use of, 144–147
  listing and evaluating sources,
    147–148
  organization of, 150–152
  plan, 143–144
  reading and taking notes, 148–150
  recopying, 155–165
  refining, 155
  revising, 155

topic choice, 142–143
Revising, 77–98
    checklist for, 101
    content, 83–85
    marking up the draft, 100
    organization, 85–88
    paragraphs, 85–94
    research paper, 155
    tips for, 78–79
Rewriting. *See* Recopying; Refining;
    Revising
Run-on sentences, 133–134

Secondary sources, 144–145
Sentence fragments, 132
Sentence outlines, 64–65
Sentences, 115–136
    clarity of, 116–118
    complex, 128–129
    compound, 127–128
    compound-complex, 128
    conciseness of, 120–123
    length of, 127
    parallel, 130–131
    periodic, 129
    run-on, 133, 134
    simple, 127
    topic, 86, 88, 95
    transitional words between, 91–93
    variation in length and structure,
        127–129
    vigorousness of, 123–126
Sexist tone, avoiding, 104–105
Slang, 102
Solution, offering a, 96
Sources
    determining kinds of, 144–145
    finding, 145–147
    identification of, 23
    listing and evaluating, 147–148
    primary, 144
    reading and taking notes on,
        148–150
    secondary, 144, 145
Spatial order, 55–58
Spelling, 132, 136

Statement of purpose, 14–16
    narrowing of, 81
    relevance of content to, 80–81
Style, 101–106
    consistency of tone and, 106
    formal, 102
    informal, 102
Subject and verb, agreement between,
    134
Subject card, in card catalog, 146
Summary of source material, 149,
    154–155

Television, as information source, 28
Tenses, consistency of, 118
Thesis. *See* Controlling idea
Thesis statement, 15, 95
Time available, choice of topic and,
    9–10
Time for writing, scheduling a reg-
    ular, 70
Title
    hook, 97
    statement, 97–98
Title page, 138
Tone, 103–106
    attitude and, 104
    consistency of style and, 106
    impersonal, 103
    personal, 103
    sexist, 104–105
Topic
    audience and, 11–13
    choice of, 7–16
    controlling idea, 15–16
    familiarity with, 9
    interest, 8
    limitations, 9–11
    narrowing, 10
    purpose, 13–15
    reading, 22–23
    relevance of, demonstration of,
        94–95
    research paper, 142–143
Topic outlines, 64
Topic sentence, 86, 88, 95

Transitional paragraphs, 92
Transitional words, 92–94
Typewritten papers, 138, 139

Verbs
    active vs. passive voice, 123–126
    agreement between subject and, 134
    "smothered," 123–124
    tenses, consistency of, 118
Visual illustrations, 44, 82
Voice, active vs. passive, 123–126

Wordiness, 102
    prepositional phrases, 122–123
Words
    abstract, 109–110
    concrete, 109–110
    connotations of, 108
    denotation of, 107
Word usage, 107–115
    appropriateness, 111–114
    precision, 107–108
    specificity, 108–109

Yearbooks, 145